'An essential read if we truly are to confront the huge challenges of modern life.'

Margaret Heffernan, TED speaker and bestselling
author of Uncharted

'A worthy reflection, particularly in light of the challenges of the coronavirus pandemic that has tested leaders globally.'

Stephen Drill, Europe Correspondent, Daily Telegraph

'Through incredibly engaging stories and compelling evidence, *Too Proud to Lead* clarifies the risks, costs, and enablers of hubris, which is paramount if leaders are to demonstrate more significant levels of collaboration, inventiveness, and trust in their careers.'

Laura Jayes, journalist and Sky News anchor

'As businesses face unprecedented uncertainty, leaders must work hard to build greater collaboration, inventiveness, and trust. *Too Proud to Lead* explains why, and in doing so, teaches leaders how to demonstrate empathy, vulnerability, and authenticity.'

Phil Benton, General Manager, Adidas

'With great power comes great responsibility. *Too Proud to Lead* is a powerful wake-up call for leaders and a reminder about how they can tap into their best selves to elevate everyone around them.'

Dorie Clark, Professor, Columbia Business School

'*Too Proud to Lead* is an indispensable guidebook for leaders who strive to unleash their organizations' intensely human, creative power.'

Michael Chavez, CEO, Duke Corporate Education

'*Too Proud to Lead* is a fantastic read that identifies hubristic leadership in action. It's essential to colleagues who struggle to find alignment with leaders and is a powerful reminder that as we become more successful, we need to be even more conscious about how our values and ethics inform our choices.'

Shaheena Janjuha-Jivraj, Associate Professor,
HEC Paris and co-author of Futureproof Your Career

'*Too Proud to Lead* is highly insightful, extraordinarily interesting, and thoroughly enlightening.'

Simon Shaw MBE, 2003 Rugby World Cup Winner

'A very insightful and engaging read – I would highly recommend it to anyone with their own business or looking to start one.'

Roger Sanchez, Grammy Award-Winning DJ and Producer

To Andrew, for introducing discernment and discipline. Your influence has been profound, and without which, this book never would have been written, so thank you, for everything.

TOO PROUD TO LEAD

How hubris can destroy effective leadership and what to do about it

Ben Laker, David Cobb and Rita Trehan

BLOOMSBURY BUSINESS
LONDON • OXFORD • NEW YORK • NEW DELHI • SYDNEY

BLOOMSBURY BUSINESS
Bloomsbury Publishing Plc
50 Bedford Square London WC1B 3DP UK
29 Earlsfort Terrace, Dublin 2, Ireland

BLOOMSBURY, BLOOMSBURY BUSINESS and the Diana logo are trademarks
of Bloomsbury Publishing Plc

First published in Great Britain 2021

A catalogue record for this book is available from the British Library

Library of Congress Cataloguing-in-Publication data has been applied for

ISBN: 978-1-4729-7303-0; eBook: 978-1-4729-7304-7

2 4 6 8 10 9 7 5 3 1

Typeset by Deanta Global Publishing Services, Chennai, India
Printed and bound in Great Britain by CPI Group (UK) Ltd, Croydon CR0 4YY

To find out more about our authors and books visit www.bloomsbury.com
and sign up for our newsletters

Contents

Foreword
by Margaret Heffernan

Success is a poor teacher. Whether in business or in life, it is impossible to analyse all of the forces that led to a positive outcome. Has my marriage proved fulfilling because I chose well, because I was lucky – or because we were never really tested by tragedy or accident? Did the business thrive because my idea was brilliant, because the people around me took a weak concept and turned it into something viable, or because my competitors lacked cash or imagination? The study of leadership is rife with attribution errors which seek to explain what cannot be proved.

But when success follows success, the easy explanation is: I did it. And the more success, the more confident that explanation appears. It is only human to begin to believe oneself invincible. That is where hubris kicks in: when imagining that one is solely responsible for one's own success.

Institutional cultures frequently make it worse. Rewards for success are large, tangible and visible: the office, the car, the lifestyle convey a potent message that a thriving organization is the fruit of one man's (or, occasionally, one woman's) labour. The human habit of hero worship amplifies a process that is deeply difficult to resist.

What gets forgotten is how many people contribute to any success, the role that luck invariably plays, the narrow escapes, the happy accidents and all the learning along the way. All are bundled into the magical property of a single person or institution – and get forgotten. That the world keeps changing compels us all to keep learning but hubris makes it feel unnecessary.

The unpredictability of contemporary life now makes hubris more dangerous than ever. Experts in forecasting argue that the best informed people – rigorous in consulting a wide range of authoritative information sources, careful to adjust their predictions, meticulous in assigning and refining probabilities and relentless in learning from their mistakes – can produce accurate forecasts only about 400 days out. For the less rigorous, the horizon for useful prediction is closer to 150 days. And even then, uncertainty remains a constant fact of life. So we have to stay alert, paying attention to the new, the inexplicable and anomalous. Reframing perspectives, listening to divergent voices, being prepared to argue and debate in order to see better and further, is a fundamental task of decision makers. Assumptions – about oneself, about the world – are dangerous; what was true yesterday might not be true today. So there can be no room for hubris in our leaders or organizations. If we are to confront the huge challenges of modern life – economic uncertainty, inequality, climate crisis – we can do so only with humility and eyes wide open.

Margaret Heffernan, TED speaker and bestselling
author of *Uncharted*
March 2021

Introduction

The word 'hubris' originates from ancient Greece. Initially used to describe behaviour that shamed or humiliated a victim, it has since evolved to describe extreme, foolish, or dangerous pride and overconfidence. Today, in the business world and in politics we recognize hubristic tendencies best by their symptoms: no prisoners taken, lack of care for others, fierce defence of reputation and power and, above all, defiant and dangerous self-interest.

Hubris is not just a danger for the person exhibiting its characteristics, but also for the people this person is tasked with leading.

We do not have to look very far to find examples of individuals and organizations displaying such tendencies; indeed evidence suggests it is spreading. The growth in usage and popularity of this phrase throughout the 2010s and into the 2020s suggests a doubling down on hubris. Doubling down is originally a gambling term, referring to a high-stakes gamble: defiance in the face of evidence and consensus. It is sticking unwaveringly to a decision or plan of action regardless of consequences or known fallout. It is an apt way to think of hubris. Tough leaders double down in the hubristic belief that listening, conceding a point, ceding or sharing power are all just signs of weakness.

The breeding ground for hubris often starts with success. It is the entry point for hubris.

The pressure for success is immense, especially in an environment where the motto is 'move fast and break things'. One success after another, builds self-confidence. But achieving more in the same way morphs self-confidence into a (false) sense of infallibility. Hubristic people can become larger than life, assuming they can do no wrong. The more an individual with 'the Midas touch' wins, the less open they are to critical feedback: why would this person need feedback when they have already cracked the code to success? Additionally, as fans and minions (descriptors they use to define other people) continue to cheer them on, hubristic individuals typically seek to feed their self-glorifying adulation tendencies. They become intensely focused on repeating their successes, seeking to make the next one even bigger and better. Finally, the individual ascends (in their minds) to a status that is seemingly invincible.

As we all climb the path towards hubris, we develop blind spots: a belief we are capable of anything, a lazy reliance on our go-to strategies and a dismissive attitude towards evidence and contrary advice.

These blind spots cause leaders to overvalue their strengths and dismiss the value that we find in continuous learning and self-reflection. It is through self-awareness and continuous learning that leaders are reminded of the need to collaborate, the role they play as a servant to their organization and the fact that they need to continually self-assess and adjust as their organization changes and the world changes around them.

Recent political history has given us a US president whose entire period in office could be characterized as one long double-down. The power concentrating in the hands of tech moguls and others is leading to double-down moments seemingly every week. The failure of so many aspects of corporate governance and a fiercely competitive global marketplace are promoting hubristic behaviour, too. And yet, as we shall see, hubris is destructive, negative and corrosive and should have no place in modern leadership.

Leadership is Everywhere

The dedication to understanding leadership has existed since humans began searching for clues about humanity and society. Research and fiction have been written, both with the goal of helping us better understand our progress as a species and the people who have led us.

We are all led by someone; by different people in different parts of our lives. Whether it is the leadership of the country that you live in, the organization in which you work, the groups or teams you associate with, or your own family, leaders within these structures have the power to push everyone forward or bring everyone down. True leadership banishes hubris and embraces collaboration, consultation, evidence and self-awareness, and yet balances that with decisiveness and urgency.

In Part 1 of this book, we explore the ways to spot the warning signs of hubris, and the conditions in which it can take hold, including some topical and pertinent case studies of hubristic behaviour. In Part 2 we offer some practical and relevant solutions, ways of developing, honing leadership and a leadership style that is inclusive, sustainable, and develops shared values and a common purpose. In short, leadership fit for the 2020s and beyond.

Part I

In the first chapter, using the case study of the Boeing 737 MAX, we illustrate how hubris can become a matter of life and death. From that high-stakes story, we then guide you through these other aspects of hubris:

Chapter 2: A Study of Hubris

This section provides a broad analysis of the warning signs of hubris in organizations. It looks at the structures which continue to enable it. We look at the corrosive effects of a lack of collaboration. Autocratic decision-making by CEOs and boards; an erosion in consultation and collaborative practices; poor collaborative examples at the top lead to more politics and silos throughout the organization; treating data as power; protecting status; rejecting outside help.

Chapter 3: The Pressure for Success

We look at institutionalized hubris and how the single-minded quest for success continues to dominate corporate culture; how financial stakeholders such as shareholders, fund managers and pension funds pursue a narrow interpretation of success; how the pressure to achieve fast results leads to an abandonment of consultation and cooperation.

Four cautionary tales: We look at four high-profile examples, each from different and important market sectors, where hubris has affected, undermined, and hollowed out highly successful companies: The We Company; General Motors; Uber; and Deutsche Bank.

Chapter 4: Walking the Hubris Tightrope

The high-profile, buccaneering CEO, with vision and drive, continues to be a model which is looked up to. The wealth, power and influence of a current crop of entrepreneurs is dizzying. Has their success been achieved by avoiding hubris by channelling the upside of determination, ambition, drive and vision? We assess the hubris balance sheet of Jobs, Zuckerberg, Bezos and Musk.

Chapter 5: The Damage Hubris Inflicts

Millions of other executives now yearn to acquire a similar megastar status to those in Chapter 4. In the process, they start to believe their own hype and seek to limit the power of others within the organization. We explore this phenomenon and highlight the key dangers and warning signs of hubristic management styles.

Part 2

Chapter 6: Balancing Collaboration with Urgency

We look at the structures needed to enable a flatter, more collaborative organization. We look at ways to ensure that decision-making and commercial agility are not compromised by the process of collaboration. We look at how to cultivate shared values and a common purpose, and give examples of agile, collaborative, purpose-driven organizations.

Chapter 7: The CEO Hubris Timeline

Examining the career arc of a CEO and how it can choose to follow the path of arrogance and hubris, or can take a different, more inclusive route. We describe the all-too recognizable journey of the flawed leader and explore ways in which the CEO, and those around that person, can avoid these pitfalls.

Chapter 8: A Better Way to Lead

This is nothing less than a description of how to be a better leader. We explore how to enable collaborative working; how to discover your purpose (and your organization's); how to create a sustainable set of values; how to serve your employees, customers and community; and how to enhance agility in a rapidly changing world.

Chapter 9: Conquering Hubris

To banish hubris takes more than rooting out an overbearing and proud CEO. It requires the organization to adopt practices and safeguards which are baked into its structure, values and purpose. Depending on the evaluation made of the current position, we show what should surely be the goal of every CEO: how to create a sustainable, hubris-free organization.

Please join us for the ride.

Part One

CHAPTER 1

Hubris: A Matter of Life and Death

Hubristic individuals are often described in a number of ways: 'self-glorifying', 'arrogant', 'insolent', 'overconfident', 'entitled', 'proud', 'overbearing', 'ignores others', 'oversteps', 'impious' or 'defying all who stand in their way'. And hubris often manifests itself in symptoms that involve losing touch with reality while at the same time overestimating one's own capabilities or competence.

While hubris is roundly, and often justifiably, condemned as a pernicious trait that undermines managers' sense of perspective and ability to make effective decisions, it is all too easy for it to take hold. If success breeds success, it can also often lead to another, more unwelcome stage, where success breeds a feeling of invincibility. Even though the mission statements of most big businesses usually include words such as 'inclusion', 'equality' and 'respect', simply saying these things doesn't make them happen. A big part of the battle against hubris is spotting it early enough to prevent it taking hold.

Hubris often results from particular sets of circumstances being in place within an organization. Either separately or cumulatively, these create a hothouse environment where it can take root, grow and spread, often as part of a distorted business culture which tacitly endorses and supports it.

Boeing 737 Max

A Matter of Life and Death, the 1946 film classic starring David Niven, is an intriguing fantasy concerning a British wartime pilot who appears to cheat death, falls in love and has to argue for his life before a celestial court. The film still retains a timeless and surreal charm, thanks to the genius of its directors, Michael Powell and Emerich Pressburger. If the movie is far-fetched, its happy ending created much-needed optimism and consolation in the face of so much devastation at the end of the Second World War.

Sadly, a real-life aviation story from the 2010s has no such happy ending. Instead, it has all the hallmarks of a Hollywood plot – a race for success; corner-cutting to win that race; arrogant management convinced they will win; cover-ups and conspiracies of silence; a sleepy and complacent regulator – all culminating in disaster.

This is the story of the Boeing 737 Max aeroplane as a plot synopsis, and perhaps one day the grim but gripping movie will be made. It is a tale of corporate and personal hubris, the consequences of which will surely continue to unravel for years to come. Most tragic of all, of course, is the terrible loss of life – 346 people died in two plane crashes, five months apart – an unprecedented pattern of failure which has left those affected outraged by the corporate complacency and arrogance at the heart of this story.

It is an instructive story with which to open this book, because, of all the industries in the world, it is aviation that is supposed to put safety ahead of any other consideration. The safety of passengers should dominate the thoughts, decisions and actions of everyone in every corner of aviation, ahead of profit, status, competitive position – everything. In doing so, those employed in that industry should demonstrate a humility in the face of the daily miracle of physics and engineering that keeps tonnes of metal safely up in the sky.

And yet it is here, tens of thousands of feet up in the air, that a series of arrogant decisions came to a head and not one, but two planes fell from the skies. The pride and hubris of Icarus could not be a more apt metaphor.

The seeds of destruction

How, in the mature, highly evolved market sector of commercial aviation, with a safety record unsurpassed by all other modes of transport, could such a disaster have occurred? Furthermore, how could it be that Boeing, the world's largest aerospace company, founded over a hundred years ago, and with more than 150,000 employees worldwide, has presided over this? Is it possible that Boeing's scale, brand, heritage and market dominance have created a hubristic corporate beast?

Let's look at how events unfolded. The story starts back in the early 2010s, when, for the first time in its history, American Airlines started to place volume orders with a European manufacturer, Airbus. Just as in the automotive industry, where US manufacturers had been slow to move away from producing gas-guzzling cars, so in aviation it was European manufacturers who were ahead of the game in producing more fuel-efficient engines. The attractiveness of this to the airlines had less to do with environmental considerations and more to do with the spectacular rise of low-cost airlines and the urgent need to cut overheads, of which fuel costs are a significant part.

The Airbus 320neo, with its low operating costs and excellent fuel efficiency, picked up hundreds of orders in 2011, which sent Boeing into a panic. Despite probably having the most well-resourced research and development department of any aerospace company, Boeing appears to have been looking the other way when the need for more fuel-efficient planes was looming on the horizon.

As a result, while American Airlines progressed its orders with Airbus, Boeing was having to play catch-up, and fast. However, 'fast' is incompatible with the usual timescale of up to 10 years that it takes to develop and produce an all-new aircraft. Initially, Boeing declared that it would embark on creating a whole new type of aircraft to suit these new market conditions. The stock markets didn't like the timing implications of that, and, in the interests of keeping the share price stable, however unwittingly, Boeing set about creating an unstable type of aircraft.

For various technical reasons, it would appear that in order to create more fuel-efficiency, new engines would need to be heavier than existing engines. The compromise, from a time-saving point of view, was to bolt this heavier engine on to a variant of an existing plane body, the 737. So, we now have an uneasy hybrid, with new, heavier engines designed to provide greater range and efficiency, fixed further forward on the wing of the plane than is the case with conventional 737s. The engineers at Boeing adapted to the anticipated problems that this might present to the handling of the plane by placing greater trust in technology rather than the pilots themselves. A new sensor was placed in the front of the plane, which would recognize changes in pitch and automatically adjust the wings to keep the plane stable. Boeing then completely changed the way in which this could be overridden by pilots, but they failed to train pilots or communicate clearly this significant change.

So, with hindsight (always a wonderful thing), we have a new aircraft with a number of significant variations from the legacy 737 models. And yet, by badging the plane as a 737 Max, it appeared to be simply a logical progression from existing tried and proven models. On this basis, Boeing took the decision not to seek recertification of this new aircraft, a decision upheld by the Federal Aviation Authority (FAA), the supposedly neutral body overseeing all aspects of US commercial aviation.

As a result of previous budget cuts, the FAA had already delegated some of its regulatory duties to the manufacturers themselves. Around a thousand Boeing employees have been seconded to the FAA, the ultimate in self-regulation. The degree to which the safety of Boeing's new design was subjected to independent rigorous scrutiny by the FAA will probably be a subject of court cases for many years to come, but what is not in dispute is that a fundamentally dangerous design of aircraft was given a licence to fly.

The fateful flights

On 29 October 2018, Lion Air flight JT610 crashes into the Java Sea, 13 minutes after take off from Jakarta airport in Indonesia. All 189 people on board are killed. The plane had been in service for less than three months. After studying the plane's black box recorder, Boeing issues updated guidance in November to pilots on how to react to readings from the plane's sensors.

Less than five months later, on 10 March 2019, an Ethiopian Airlines Boeing 737 Max crashes six minutes after taking off from Addis Ababa. All 157 people on board are killed. In both cases, sensors had automatically pushed the nose of the plane downwards to avoid stalling, with tragic consequences. The pilots had been unable to take control of the aircraft even though there is evidence of frantic wrestling with the plane's controls.

Three days after this second accident, Boeing grounded its entire fleet of 737 Max aircraft, and, almost two years on there was still much debate over whether the aircraft should still be in the air at all. In November 2020 the 737 Max was cleared to resume flights in North America and Brazil, but aviation authorities in several other areas, including Canada and Europe, were considering the issue into early 2021. In the meantime, it is estimated that the immediate cost to Boeing is $19 billion and the rival that it sought to outmanoeuvre, Airbus, looks set to overtake it as the world's largest aerospace company.

The fallout

Boeing's CEO Dennis Muilenburg was ousted in December 2019 and, although he forfeited stock worth $14.6 million, he still walked away with a package of stock and pension awards worth over $60 million. In the meantime, the ripple effect of the 737 grounding right across the US aerospace supply chain is severe, with layoffs and losses in many interconnected companies. Indeed, according to US government figures, the effect of all this has been so significant that it has had a demonstrable impact on the entire US economy. As a postscript, in January 2021, Boeing was charged with fraud and conspiracy by the US Justice Department with regard to the 737 Max scandal, and fined $2.5 billion.

A perfect storm of arrogance

The Watergate scandal of the early 1970s started as a bungled break-in of the Democratic National Committee headquarters in Washington DC, but what brought down President Nixon were the lies and the cover-up that followed. In the same way, it is the cover-ups and deceit surrounding the circumstances of the introduction of the 737 Max which are the most shocking part of this story.

Internal Boeing messages and emails between Boeing employees working on the project, from 2015 to 2018, have revealed a culture of flippancy towards safety and the FAA, as well as recognizing the engine problem well before the crashes. The reaction to the first crash, given that the company was aware of the design flaws, should have been an immediate grounding of all 737 Max aircraft. Instead, possible pilot error was floated as a reason, with confusing guidance then being issued. Nearly five months were allowed to pass before the final admittance of the scale of the problem, with those further 157 lives being needlessly lost in the second crash.

A perfect storm led to the tragedy of the 737 Max: Boeing's arrogance borne out of its status as market leader, the neutering of the FAA as industry overseer, a commercial rush to react to Airbus, a trust in technology over pilots, and a culture which had lost sight of safety as being the number one consideration. Arrogance and a sense of invincibility were evident throughout Boeing. At board level, in the design and manufacturing teams, in the software teams, in the testing and the marketing of this aircraft, there was a blindness, perhaps even a wilful blindness, driven by selfish and narrow commercial considerations.

Institutionalized hubris

All this represents institutionalized hubris and, at the time of writing, the full extent of the consequences for Boeing are still playing out. To succeed in aerospace, your brand and your reputation must be built on the foundation stone of one thing: trust. Millions of people each year, all around the world, entrust their lives to aircraft manufacturers; that trust is hard won and easily lost. The lid has been lifted on the true internal culture at Boeing and it has been found wanting. For Boeing this is now not a simple technical fix, a software fault which can be easily remedied. This has been exposed as a sacrifice of safety on the altar of short-term commercial advantage – a true case of a matter of life and death.

This Boeing story, then, has the highest stakes possible; in some of the other studies of hubris later in this book the stakes are lower but no less instructive. In this age of corporate governance, regulatory checks and balances, executive and non-executive oversight, how can shortcuts and evasiveness ride roughshod over an entire industry's failsafe measures? These are eighteenth-century mine owners' attitudes exposed in a sleek twenty-first-century corporation. This is an above-the-law stance borne out of ... **hubris**.

CHAPTER 2

A Study of Hubris

In 2009, a group of researchers overseen by senior faculty from Kingston University, Duke Corporate Education, London Business School and the University of Oxford undertook a study looking at hubristic personality changes in 400 leaders from 160 organizations spread over eight years. The team analysed the leaders' beliefs, education, actions, experiences and recognition, using eight yardsticks by which to develop a better understanding of their actions, sometimes even three years after they had left their particular roles.

Leaders were selected for the study based on having similar Key Performance Indicators (KPIs), responsibilities and abilities (to manage costs, revenues and stakeholders). The study itself encompassed both real-time observations of leaders at work, as well as access to each company's management systems, which housed valuable organizational data. All information was provided in a non-identifiable way. Researchers were able to analyse key data reference points, including staffing levels, workloads, commentary from induction and exit interviews, and relevant background data, such as staff's CVs. As well as considering organizational and people data, the researchers also reviewed financial and performance data and governance reports. Visits were made four to six times annually to each organization. During these visits, the 400 leaders were interviewed in an effort to shed light on their actions as well as to understand the underlying rationale behind those actions. In addition, researchers interviewed a number of people who had worked with these leaders, in order to gain insight and clarity concerning the measures taken, the underlying rationale for those decisions, as well as their results and impacts.

By observing changes in personality over time exhibited by these leaders, researchers in this study were able to identify various sources of hubris, many of which led some of these individuals to believe that they were infallible. In many cases this resulted in them behaving in ways which demonstrated excessive pride, which held the potential to lead ultimately to their downfall.

Bosses, not leaders

It is often only after the leader's reign has ended that organizations can look back and identify hubris and assess the fallout. The word 'leader' will be used throughout this book more as a job title as opposed to a style of management. However, what a telling difference exists between 'boss' and 'leader'.

'Boss' has a mid-twentieth-century ring to it, the overbearing and tyrannical figure of Hollywood cliché. And yet it is still used, often in very different ways depending on the setting and the context, and indeed the gender. All too often, in unguarded comments in offices in the 2020s, an insidious 'y' is added to the word when applied to female managers. Men are 'the boss' and women are 'bossy'; the former a term of admiration for being in command, leading from the front, being in control. Women who take control in the same way are undermined and sniped at, that pejorative adjectival 'y' changing the management style to a hectoring, nagging, annoying persistence in demanding that things move in a certain direction. It's an attitude that should be as extinct as the dinosaur, but it is not quite yet confined to office dinosaurs. And, depressingly, sometimes the users of the term are female employees.

But back to 'boss' versus 'leader'. At times of crisis, high risk or a threat from external forces such as a sudden hostile takeover bid, a company will look to the CEO to step up to the plate and show the hostile bidder who is boss. In such circumstances there may not be time for the niceties of consultation and inclusive involvement of all stakeholders. The markets reopen the next morning and unless a decisive strategy and statement can be put together and issued, market traders will have decided the company's fate before anything else can be done. In those high-pressure, high-stakes circumstances you need a leader who is also prepared to be the boss, exhibit bold, decisive thinking, and to articulate that in interviews in a way which displays total confidence and determination. In these situations, only the strong survive, even if a massive game of bluff may be involved.

So, in boss mode, our CEO pulls that one off, saves the day, and brushes aside the retrospective concerns of those who weren't consulted or involved in the weekend's decisions and briefings. Triumphs like this can be horribly beguiling. Our heroic CEO is enjoying this new status and the adrenalin rush it brings, loving being the focus of media attention, and the precedent of being able to act and succeed in a way that bypasses the standard boardroom approval conventions.

This is power in its purest form, beholden to no one (in that moment), with the triumph of being the main decision-maker. These are the moments when confidence can tip over into overconfidence; when being inclusive and consultative feels an unnecessary bore and a counterproductive slowing down of great decision-making. The external hostile takeover is replaced by a hostile internal takeover – by the CEO. Steering committees and consultation groups are quietly dismantled, or their next meetings become endlessly postponed. Direct access to the CEO becomes more difficult, except for a tight inner circle. Our hero starts to believe that bold decisions are the way to solve everything and a series of previously unannounced 'initiatives' start to emanate from the CEO's office. The ways in which this power grab can manifest itself are many and varied; some subtle and gradual, some startling and immediate. Swept along by the recent triumph, it's amazing what can get pushed through in the sudden euphoria. Boss-mode becomes a permanent state and true leadership recedes. In politics, electorates often seem to admire bold, wrong-headed action rather than slower, more considered decisions. But can the same be said in Corporate World?

Hubris: its stealthy arrival

Glance at the CV of any CEO and you will usually see an impressive track record. Shake hands with them and they exude confidence and an apparent knack for taking well-calculated risks. But follow the trail left behind them and you may well find examples of hubris in their wake.

Unfortunately for recruiters and board members, all too often there will be no detectable sign of hubris when that leader is hired. In fact, many of the qualities that have been sought out and form the basis for hiring the new leader may well include the seeds of hubris; there is often a fine line when dividing a leadership quality from its darker side. Organizations hire leaders who are successful, confident, charismatic and clear-minded in their goals and objectives. How easy is it for those qualities to tip over into their counterproductive opposites: overconfidence, single-mindedness, arrogance and even bullying? Looking at the results of the 2009 study, the answer is: all too easily. Success can lead to a feeling of infallibility. The usual reward for success is promotion, often to a role where theoretical accountability increases – the buck stops here. But often accountability to peers falls away, as, the higher they climb, the fewer peers they have around them. This results in fewer and fewer people in place to monitor their thinking, decisions, strategies and actions. Peers have become subordinates and, looking upwards, they can see that their leader has developed hubris, as they are able to contrast attitudes, style of management and access to that person with the better days when that person was merely a peer who was going places. Now the leader is out of reach, too powerful to confront, and those former peers become reluctant to speak out for fear of retribution.

There may even be a more manipulative process taking place. Successful, confident leaders often start to believe their own hype, their early successes leading to a feeling that they have a unique and special touch. This can become an addictive, beguiling state in which to find oneself and a state that can be reinforced and perpetuated by ensuring that the specialness of your touch is not questioned. One of the ways in which this can be achieved is to appoint in your immediate downline those managers who seem most impressed with you and who ask few, if any, awkward questions.

Perhaps unsurprisingly, we see this type of selection process happening all the time with politicians. Presidents and prime ministers conduct reshuffles, which remove any awkward-squad types – i.e., those politicians who articulate the 'yes, but'-type queries which we, as voters, are all shouting at the TV news. In their place are installed ministers and 'advisers' who say what the leader wants to hear, toe the party line to the letter and who therefore, collectively, focus on policies and a style of government which serve themselves and their party ahead of their country. Sounds familiar? Of course it does, hence the disenchantment and cynicism with politics and elected politicians across the democratic world.

That level of manipulation and self-serving is, unfortunately, far from unknown in the boardroom. CEOs making a series of appointments (that in themselves immediately create an indebtedness) in their own image is all too common. A boardroom in the 2020s should increasingly display a diversity and a breadth of background, outlook and opinion. If it doesn't consist of a healthy gender and ethnic diversity, then that may be an early indication of the board being formed in the image of its maker – i.e., its CEO. A middle-aged white male CEO surrounded by other middle-aged white males is a 'Meet the Board' annual report photo we've all seen too many times in the past 50 years. While gender and ethnic diversity is no guarantee of a plurality of opinion, with the resultant potential for healthy checks and balances to the power of the CEO, it's likely to be, at the very least, a positive starting point.

Boardroom style

The way in which boards operate and communicate can be highly instructive, and an effective bellwether of the CEO's attitude to power, inclusiveness and delegation. If it is one where all the decisions and announcements are exclusively delivered and communicated by the CEO, with barely a reference to any other board members, this may well be a further warning sign of the presence of hubris.

'X Corporation embroiled in bitter boardroom row' screams a business press headline. That is never going to be seen as a positive PR message to the world. It indicates a failure to agree on policy, on strategy, on the direction and vision for the business, all of which make stakeholders nervous. But is it entirely negative? For sure, if the disagreement gets to the point where it is a 'row' and the corporation is 'embroiled' in it (seemingly the only context in which this strange word is used), then relationships may well have broken down and any constructive dialogue may have been drowned out by politics and personalities.

However, if internal disagreements in the boardroom still take place but are kept within those four walls until some sort of outcome can be agreed, that is surely a sign of healthy checks and balances being in place to keep the CEO himself in check. A CEO who encourages constructive criticism in the boardroom (and elsewhere, which we discuss later) is one who has put in place their own anti-hubris strategies. Is your boardroom a forum for healthy debate in which all voices are listened to and respected? Or are board meetings merely a top-down communication of the CEO's thinking and decisions, with the meeting often just a rubber-stamping exercise? Or, more subtly, that an apparent listening process occurs, but original plans and decisions put forward by the CEO are never significantly altered, even after 'taking on board' what has been said by others. 'Taking it on board' – what an insidious phrase that has become. Politicians use it all the time as a deflection from actually listening and acting upon legitimate concerns. Along with 'respecting your views', which almost always means the exact opposite, both phrases are inevitably followed by a 'but' and then a reversion to the person's original viewpoint, with no real accommodation of the views of others.

In the current era, it is this 'wolf in sheep's clothing' style of autocratic leadership that is far more common than the Victorian mill or pit owner's habit of proprietorial management. Nowadays, old-style autocracy is found out and prevented from rising to the top far more often. The hubris radar in organizations is more finely tuned, ensuring that good old-fashioned bullies will find it harder to make it to the top. No: they are smarter than that, creating a veneer of inclusion, of listening, of consensual behaviour, while all the time doing no more than paying lip service to such practices. If, as a manager, you experience a steady cycle of elation at being listened to, followed by a nagging disappointment that the follow-through never quite happened in the way that it was initially promised, then you have been a victim of classic 'taking it on board' tactics.

By bringing people along in this faux-consensual manner, the power base of this wolf CEO grows, creating an even more dominant position by appearing to do the reverse. All the other sheep are now in the pen with the wolf, and at its mercy. Anyone attempting to call out such a CEO as being autocratic and non-consensual is then seen by others as being a troublemaker with their own political agenda, rather than the one person with the courage to speak out. At that point the boss disguised as leader is as one, and thus the illusion is complete.

The cult of personality

Compared with executives from the 1950s and even through to the 1990s, modern CEOs are visible media personalities. Unlike their older counterparts, who were mostly unknown and unrecognized by anyone outside the company, many of today's executives are front and centre on every social media platform in existence. They tweet their own opinions, blog frequently and show up on Facebook and in the comments of articles on LinkedIn. The executives of our parents and grandparents shunned the press, and only provided prepared statements carefully created by in-house PR departments.

Modern CEOs write books, use publicists, promulgate personal philosophies and grant access to media interviews. Even the ordinary citizen who has no interest in business, entrepreneurship, fame or fortune knows who they are. Who wouldn't? Their faces adorn every newspaper and magazine, often well away from the business sections. If seeing their faces in magazines wasn't enough, they're also on YouTube, giving keynote speeches and being interviewed on the evening news about the issues that shape our public and private agendas. They criticize lawmakers about investing public money, and they even stand up to be arrested in public protests. People respect them for their views on things unrelated to businesses, such as the best places to visit for vacation or the appropriate attire to wear when speaking to their followers. Ask anyone, for instance, what Steve Jobs wore or what Mark Zuckerberg wears, and they will almost certainly be able to tell you (jeans and black turtlenecks, and jeans and short-sleeved grey t-shirts, respectively). Today's CEO isn't just a name and a face: they're a brand. And they're encouraging others to be brands, too. We're becoming a society known more for our brand and less for our character. And that's often where the problem of hubris begins.

In Chapter 4 we will explore four of the biggest personal brands: Jobs, Zuckerberg, Bezos and Musk (no first name or business brand link required: we all know who they are and which brands they are associated with). Each of these has walked or is walking the hubris tightrope and we will consider where each of them might sit on the hubris spectrum.

Looking beyond these big figures to less household names, every industry or sector has its big hitters, its 'Oh, he/she's on the news AGAIN' people whose publicists have ensured they are the default person called up for a comment on the latest topical development in their sector, often unrelated directly to their corporation or organization. They are the experts, the opinion-setters, the gurus, the self-appointed spokesperson for an entire industry. The hype becomes self-perpetuating, fuelled by a media looking for quick, easily obtained comment and copy on any particular issue. It's so easy, and frankly understandable, for this to go to the person's head, for them to come to believe their own hype all too readily. With 24-hour news outlets to fill, business activity, initiatives, takeovers, mergers, rumours of takeovers and mergers are all picked over and analysed in ways that even 20 years ago would be unrecognizable. A story which in the past warranted a brief column on page seven of the *Financial Times* becomes, for a 12-hour window at least, a rolling financial news item attracting 'what if' punditry and commentary.

Into the grateful, hungry maws of this media machine jumps the attention-seeking, hubristic CEO, eager to grab every media opportunity as yet another way to cultivate and develop their personal brand. Social media has given every one of us an awareness of the power and responsibility of our personal brand. Whether we want it or not, we all have one; we just differ in the degree we choose to promote and exploit it. For the egotistical CEO, the combined opportunity of social media and an insatiable news machine has created the perfect 'look at me' platform, available 24 hours a day, 365 days of the year.

Spiralling rewards

A major contributor to CEOs' inflated sense of worth is their almost universally inflated net worth. CEO reward inflation is dizzying and a growing and understandable source of discontent, both within organizations and in wider society. In many developed Western economies, governments are beginning to sit up and take notice of this, introducing legislation that demands more transparency on levels of executive pay and its relationship to average median pay.

In 2019, the non-profit think-tank the Economic Policy Institute (www.epi.org) conducted an analysis of the top 350 US companies. It estimated that the ratio of CEO pay in relation to that of an average employee's wages was at just 21:1 in 1965 but had spiralled to an incredible 320:1 just over 50 years later, in 2019. Has the average value of the input by CEOs to these 350 companies risen by a similar percentage, i.e. just under 1,500 per cent, in the same period? Since this increase far outstrips gains in stock prices and corporate profits across the same period, the answer has to be no.

If the publication of these pay ratios in the US, the UK and elsewhere was supposed to shame pay reward committees and CEOs into a period of greater pay restraint, there are precious few signs of this taking hold. Executive compensation company Equilar (https://insight.equilar.com), which has even developed an executive pay tracker app, studied the tech sector in particular and found that tech CEO salaries rose 15 per cent in 2018 versus 2017, looking at a sample of the 3,000 largest US tech companies. In the same period, average median pay across the tech sector in fact declined by 2 per cent. With that average figure sitting at a reasonably healthy $82,500 (compared to many other sectors), average CEO salaries sat at 129 times higher than that.

When Wall Street exploded in the 1980s, Tom Wolfe's novel *Bonfire of the Vanities* referred to all the ambitious young traders as 'Masters of the Universe'. That sense of infallibility and impregnability was fuelled by unprecedented financial rewards, which accelerated at rates never seen before. Sound familiar? In the same way, these obscene (yes, let's call it out) levels of CEO pay, both in absolute terms and in ratio terms, all too easily give rise to a new breed of Masters of the Universe. If you are earning more than 100 times the average salary of workers in your business, it's all too easy to believe that you are 100 times more valuable (in every sense) than those around you. The organization must think that you are considerably more important if they are paying you that much, right? Executive pay review boards are complicit in this crazy inflation, as the trickle-down effect is that the reward packages of its members, if not at the lofty levels of the CEO, have some sort of ratio relationship to it and keep moving upwards at the same time. Institutional shareholders are often reluctant to rock the boat either, leaving patchy and rarely-heard individual shareholder revolts at AGMs to make little impact in the news. The gravy train keeps rolling, with companies seeing a high CEO reward package as a halo indicator of status, success and confidence in the business.

In other words, if the whole reward structure has loosened its bearings with reality, what chance does the CEO have of retaining a grounded ego? Money buys status and a lifestyle, which constantly reinforces self-importance and a sense of being special. Workplace advisers and a small army of support staff are swapped for a similar structure at home, all eager to please and satisfy every whim and desire. Teams that are paid to say 'yes' to every request in a domestic setting can become easily confused with the expected response from workplace associates. In this rarefied bubble, it must be almost impossible to retain a sense of perspective and humility in one's everyday dealings.

From gated estates to chauffeured cars to penthouse offices, CEOs can remain untroubled by the voices and concerns of regular workers, indeed of regular people full stop. All this isn't the politics of envy, it's simply an examination of the circumstances in which a CEO can lose a sense of perspective of their own worth, of the value of their talents. There is no problem with rewarding success, wealth and employment creation by a truly gifted entrepreneur. And there are many of those out there, risk-takers who are ultimately responsible for the livelihoods of tens of thousands of people in their organization and its supply chain. For this elite, the positive effect of their talents, when costed up, can make their reward package look good value. But these people represent a minority.

Rewarding failure

As an instructive example in a sphere away from CEOs in businesses, let's look at football managers in the English Premier League. With over £1 billion in revenue, the competition is the most lucrative football league in the world. You would imagine that to be the manager – in this case, let's call the position the equivalent of a CEO – of any of the 20 clubs in the Premier League you would need an impeccable CV of success. In fact, quite the reverse seems to be the case. Let's look at one Premier League manager, Roy Hodgson, currently at Crystal Palace in south London on a salary in excess of £2.5 million. His is a career of exceptional longevity: 44 years as a top-level manager, starting in 1976 at underperforming Halmstads BK in Sweden. He spent five years in this formative position and lifted Halmstads to win the Swedish league twice. Indeed, Hodgson says of this, 'my greatest achievement would have to be the water-into-wine job at Halmstads BK'. On the back of this achievement, itself from a long-past era in football, Hodgson has managed more than 20 different teams, including various national sides. Since the Halmstads days, however, Hodgson has failed to win a league trophy with any top teams or any tournaments with national sides, including England.

This example of a revolving door of managerships, including five outright sackings, is commonplace in the Premier League, with Hodgson's the most notable for its length as a managerial career. Is the gene pool for those qualified to be top-flight managers, notwithstanding every club having a ballooning backroom staff operation, really that small? It would appear so. Whenever the frequent vacancies pop up at a Premier League club, sometimes more than once in the same season as impatience for results grows, the same revolving door of candidates comes into play. Some of them have managed the same club more than once, returning after an ignominious sacking at some point in the past. Have they no pride?

All this is played out very publicly in the sports pages of the UK media and so it is an instructive example very much in the public domain. Inflation in managers' remuneration packages, and the yawning gap between these and that of some of the club's staff (though not the players, of course, whose pay is even more stellar), is not dissimilar to that in large companies. The same managers keep being hired because their CV of club positions grants them a unique level of credibility with the clubs' boards and their fanbase. Breaking into this privileged circle is remarkably difficult and, once in, being permanently excluded from it seems to be equally as difficult. Keep losing to keep winning!

A similarly exclusive club has developed in the world of being a CEO. Having the experience of being CEO of a top company is rare, and companies prefer to recruit people who already have that experience rather than promoting someone to their first CEO-ship. And so it becomes a simple case of supply and demand. With a limited pool of proven CEOs, they can name their price, and on the evidence of reward package inflation, clearly do, with some ambition.

And what of their CVs? Are they any better than Roy Hodgson's? Well, too many seem to rely on past triumphs long after their relevance has passed. Of the CEOs you know, who is still talking about their equivalent of pulling up Halmstads BK from the threat of relegation to winning the league, over 40 years ago? Just as in our previous example of boss-like behaviour winning the day once and then defining the preferred style of management, so too can a past triumph be proudly wheeled out on multiple occasions in front of different CEO selection panels, its significance and value stretched to breaking point. In specific sectors and markets, such triumphs take on mythic status: the daring takeover; the thrillingly innovative product; the creation of a whole new market sector; or the mould-breaking market model. Boards are beguiled into appointing an industry legend, when often that 'legend' status should be ringing alarm bells. All too often, legends believe their own hype, usually acquired decades earlier when market conditions made it considerably easier to create such memorable impacts in a particular sector. In today's mature, developed, global markets, achieving paradigm-shifting results is way more difficult, and yet boards hope that a legend taking the helm will rekindle the magic which was there when the company first started and had its key Big Idea.

In these hothouse conditions of astonishing levels of reward and a revolving door of the CEO elite, it's all too easy and understandable for the individuals lucky enough to be in these posts to take on an exaggerated view of their own importance and value.

According to research conducted in 2017 by Crist Kolder, a Chicago-based executive search firm, the average age of new CEOs and CFOs at the US's biggest companies increased in the five years between 2012 and 2017. It has moved from 45 years old to 50 for CEOs and from 42 to 48 for CFOs. The study looked at 673 companies in the Fortune 500 and S&P 500. Not quite as old as our warhorse Roy Hodgson at 73, but, for all the talk of young guns taking over tech companies and others, this points to a continuation of an old boy network.

And that's just the figure for *new* CEOs and CFOs – the average age of all in-post CEOs is notably higher than that. Consulting firm Korn Ferry found that in 2017 the average age for a CEO across all sectors was 58, even older in financial services, at 60. The vast majority of these are white men. According to a Pew Research Center analysis of S&P 500 companies, only just over 5 per cent of CEOs in 2017 were women, although this was an improvement on the 3 per cent figure a decade earlier. The number of black CEOs is vanishingly small and shrinking, with Korn Ferry reporting that the figure in 2019 is four, down from seven in 2009.

So, this world of the CEO in the US and other Western economies is an exclusive club dominated by older white men, a hegemony which will take some shifting, its power embedded firmly in our business culture.

As with the comments about pay ratios, this is not a rant at old white men (OK, perhaps it is a little …) so much as a pinpointing of where our hubris breeding ground resides. Self-satisfied, self-serving, conservative and unchallenged – what better conditions for hubris to take hold and thrive? Threats to the status quo have come and gone: the counter-culture of the 1960s; the displacement of traditional industries by the dotcom boom; the volatility of successive financial booms and crashes; the democratization of commerce through online trading; globalization; and environmentalism. All these and more have failed to disrupt significantly the traditional pyramid structures of large corporations, and as the pay ratio statistics indicate, the pyramid is becoming sharper, not flatter.

The grip of an elite on the levers of power in Western commerce is now tighter than ever before. A lack of diversity and plurality, combined with a rewards structure that often has the unintended consequence of rewarding failure – as we've already discussed in Chapter 1, with the massive severance payment to the Boeing CEO – do nothing to remedy the situation. As a result, the need is now stronger than ever to create corporate environments where CEO accountability is more rigorously enforced; where a democratization of power is encouraged; and where the culture is one of co-operation and collaboration and not top-down decision-making from a small, powerful elite. The steps needed to move in that direction will be covered in subsequent chapters.

CHAPTER 3

The Pressure for Success

Institutionalized hubris

Is hubris within corporations the result of a few rogue individuals with extreme character traits abusing their power? In a handful of examples this may be the case, but most of the time it is enabled and even sanctioned by the whole structure of corporate business. The primacy of ever-upward quarterly results and the shareholder being the dominant stakeholder create an environment where short-termism and the quick win continue to be rewarded. It is here that overconfidence and success at any price find their natural home.

Quarterly reporting encourages short-termism

Quarterly reporting by public companies remains a statutory requirement in the US, although it was suspended within the EU in 2014, at which time the UK abandoned the mandating of it. However, to keep in line with Wall Street expectations, many EU-based multinationals continue with quarterly reporting to follow the US example.

In some ways, quarterly reporting is a force for good. It can be argued that it is a mechanism that increases transparency, as, under law, quarterly reports are sworn to be true and therefore have been scrutinized and approved by lawyers and accountants prior to being released. Investors, analysts and fund managers welcome quarterly reporting as a near-constant feed of information on the state of the companies that form the elements of their investment portfolios.

However, these benefits of increased oversight are overshadowed by its encouragement of a culture that is short-termist and narrow in its outlook, keeping a business and its board focused on the treadmill of earnings-per-share results. The narrower the agenda that a CEO and board choose to focus on, the less inclusive and collaborative they need to be. When collaboration and consultation, key tools in pursuing wider and longer-term objectives, are marginalized, it only becomes easier for the agenda of individuals to flourish.

A new paradigm

Back in 2016, the World Economic Forum's International Business Council published *The New Paradigm*, which was somewhat wordily sub-titled: 'A Roadmap for an Implicit Corporate Governance Partnership Between Corporations and Investors to Achieve Sustainable Long-Term Investment and Growth'. For our purposes, the key phrases in that title were 'Corporate Governance Partnership' and 'Sustainable Long-Term Investment and Growth'. *The New Paradigm* is available to download from weforum.org.

What it identifies is that there is a pressing need (even more so now than in 2016) for a wider agenda to be adopted by business corporations in order to ensure the long-term success of the business *and* all relevant stakeholders: shareholders, employees, suppliers and the wider community. We will explore further in Part 2 how a more sustainable, responsible approach can only succeed by being a fully participatory programme involving all these stakeholders and how this widening of the objectives for businesses does, by necessity, involve a widening, too, of scrutiny, governance and the responsibilities of a senior team. All these are the enemies of and antidote to hubris, killing it before it can take root.

Buy-back success

Although this agenda is constructive and healthy, we are not there yet and, while that remains the case, hubristic behaviour can still take hold. The notorious example of General Electric's (GE) former

CEO Jeff Immelt is instructive in studying the ill effects of a narrow, ultimately selfish agenda. In 2016/17, Immelt went on a $24 billion spending spree, buying back GE stock at what then turned out to be extremely high prices. Instead of creating the attractive proposition to shareholders of making shares scarcer and making profitability look better, this action diminished GE's ability to invest in new projects and just added to its (at the time) considerable debt mountain. Most of these billions were spent on buying shares when the price was in excess of $30 per share. During 2020 the share price fell to a low of $5.50; at the start of 2021 it was sitting at just over a third of that buy-back price (around $11). The fallout has seen GE slash its dividend, divest itself of some profitable long-term businesses as part of a $200 billion sell-off and lay off staff in considerable numbers.

The reasons for GE's ongoing difficulties are complex and varied and cannot all be laid at the door of the buy-back decision. But the compulsion to prop up the share price, with the nice added bonus of being able to exercise executive share options at a sweet-spot moment in the buy-back process, is a driver of short-termist decision-making. With share ownership still sitting in a general 80:20 ratio (i.e. 80 per cent of shares owned by 20 per cent of the population), it remains a mechanism that concentrates influence and wealth in the hands of an elite. Is that elite too powerful? CEO Immelt's power allowed him to conduct a strategy at GE that was highly damaging and ultimately led to his removal, but not before some tactics were employed which the business is still in the process of recovering from.

If Immelt and his behaviour were enabled, and even encouraged and sanctioned, by the traditional conventions and instruments of the financial markets and its zeal for great quarterly results, they are by no means unique.

Four cautionary tales

Following on from the Boeing example in Chapter 1, we will now explore four more examples from the past few years of hubristic decision-making. While the corporate excesses of the 1980s and 1990s may have been curbed to some degree by greater regulation and governance, there are still contemporary examples from which we learn.

Each of these is from a different and significant market sector, where hubris, either on a systemic level across the organization or driven largely by high-profile CEOs, has affected, undermined and hollowed out some previously highly successful companies. In doing so, we use these tales to contextualize hubris and the pathway towards it. Following which, within Part 2, we will offer some practical advice on avoiding hubris and dealing with it.

Tale 1: WeWork

The name of this company and its various sectors (WeWork, WeGrow and WeLive) can now be seen through a lens of irony: it is a failure to embrace the true open and collaborative spirit that 'We' suggests, and has caused co-founder Adam Neumann to experience one of the most spectacular falls from grace in recent corporate history.

The concept and purpose of WeWork is not particularly new and far from unique. WeWork is simply an office-leasing company that makes money from renting office space, a service which has been around almost as long as people have worked in offices. WeWork's spin on this is to create a community feel to it by focusing on offering shared office space, ideal for freelancers, start-ups and remote workers in search of an occasional base away from a home office. It plays up the potential networking opportunities of these shared spaces and creates designated spaces within each block to facilitate this. All offered in a range of great-value flexible packages to individuals and small businesses, with office costs effectively shared across a large number of people.

Understandably, this proved popular. As a (literally) bricks and mortar business, it needed to demonstrate some real distinctiveness, purpose and value to grow and to attract investors. In this way, it differs from many other stratospheric start-ups which have nothing to show investors other than an idea, an app, some coders and a load of enthusiasm.

All great ideas are, at heart, simple ones, and Neumann's quickly found favour with investors. Here was a way to unlock the value of underperforming office spaces languishing in every city, even in hotspots such as New York.

The power of We

The success and growth of WeWork went to the head of its co-founder, who was just 31 when WeWork was launched in 2010. When he first moved to New York in 2001, Neumann lived in a tiny apartment, a situation he has long since moved on from. Even in his wildest dreams at that point, Neumann couldn't have anticipated in 2018 becoming, as WeWork did, Manhattan's single biggest office tenant. Though this title was lost one year later, there's no doubt his journey from that small apartment to his zenith – the decision to go public with WeWork – was impressive and rapid, but the extent to which his self-belief became distanced from reality can be seen in that stock offer.

The first two sentences in the prospectus summary within the company's paperwork for the initial public offering (IPO) of shares were: 'We are a community company committed to maximum global impact. Our mission is to elevate the world's consciousness.' Reading that, you realize you are looking at a very special company and a CEO with a unique vision. All-encompassing in its ambition; utterly meaningless in its purpose.

It was this document, issued in August 2019, which gave potential investors their first insight into the financial details of WeWork. The problem was that it revealed, beyond the new-age slogans and the guru-like hype surrounding Neumann, that financially this was a dysfunctional business. Losses counted in billions; a labyrinth of leases on buildings and some scary future lease obligations; and plans to double down on these issues by expanding aggressively – these were the realities behind the slogans. 'The more locations we strategically cluster in a given city, the larger and more dynamic our community becomes' was another bold proclamation, with no explanation of the value of 'dynamic' forthcoming.

Neumann started to believe he had a messianic mission, way beyond the humdrum business of renting office space. 'There are 150 million orphans in the world. We want to solve this problem and give them a new family: the WeWork family.' He is reported to have made this statement to his staff at a company party in 2018. The IPO prospectus referred to 'Adam' 169 times, the whole empire centring around him.

'We dedicate this to the power of We—greater than any one of us, but inside each of us' was another statement in the IPO document. Well, in the years leading up to that point, WeWork had accumulated over $8 billion of debt, across a number of leading banks. It stated that it had minimum future lease obligations of $47 billion stretching over the next 15 years. Included in these lease obligations were a number of properties that Neumann had bought and was then leasing back to WeWork, making millions of dollars in the process. So this 'power of We' was in reality the 'power of Me', Neumann himself, to conduct business that included flagrant conflicts of interest.

A denial of democracy

All this was strengthened by the use of dual-class stock structures. According to the *Wall Street Journal*, in 2014 WeWork's investors created a new dual-class of stock for Neumann, one that gave him all the voting power on policy issues, with little or none left in the hands of ordinary investors. He had demanded that each of his shares should carry 20 times the voting power of ordinary shares. There was a backlash against this which forced Neumann to eventually reduce this to just three times that of other investors. This use of dual-class stock as a way of holding on to power in the face of tiresome investor democracy is on the rise, particularly in the tech sector, and it is creating the perfect conditions for the hubristic CEO to thrive.

The positive gloss put on dual-class stock is that it frees up CEOs from the concerns we have outlined above, of the quarterly reporting treadmill. The rationale goes that by insulating leaders from the day-to-day concerns of standard stock price rises and falls, these visionary CEOs can concentrate on fulfilling the long-term vision of the business. Both Google and Facebook have adopted this structure, for the benefit of their founders.

Snap, of Snapchat fame, when it went public in 2018, issued shares to regular shareholders that carried no voting rights at all. As a sign of that dismantling of even a pretence of a plurality of voices, Snap didn't even bother to hold a formal shareholder annual meeting. All power is instead in the hands of Snap CEO Evan Spiegel and Snap's co-founder Robert Murphy. Between them, they control almost 94 per cent of the votes at the company.

But back to Neumann and WeWork. In a prophetic encounter, Neumann's wife, Rebekah Paltrow Neumann (cousin of Gwyneth Paltrow), has recalled that on their first date she called out Neumann as being 'full of shit'. This might have been a noteworthy caveat for all those banks and investors to bear in mind when they piled their money into WeWork.

For a while, however, it all worked brilliantly. At its height, WeWork had operations in 111 cities across 29 countries. It was all WeWorking so brilliantly that up until the IPO it looked as if Neumann was all set to realize a personal stake of up to $14 billion from the flotation. This would have catapulted him into the top 100 of the Bloomberg rankings of the world's richest people. Along the way Neumann had already acquired five luxury homes across the US and in his native Israel. Jet-setting around the world in his private Gulfstream jet to attend celebrity parties, he appeared to be living the dream: the rock and roll lifestyle of the self-styled visionary entrepreneur.

Neumann becomes Icarus

As we will see later with Bezos and Musk, there comes a point where the boundaries of the earth seem a little constricting for one's ambition; Neumann has spoken in the past of setting up WeWork Mars, no doubt its shared office space supplied by Amazon and accessed via Tesla vehicles. Politics also interested him, although limiting himself to the US would clearly be a little parochial. Running for 'president of the world' was more in his sights.

Within the business, he began to display all the traits of a quixotic dictator. He would make sudden intemperate decisions such as imposing, without warning or rationale, a company-wide ban on meat. He saw nothing wrong in selling the trademark to 'We' to his own company for around $6 million, money back into his own pocket for his own company's asset.

All this made Neumann a beguiling and fascinating figure to the business media and beyond, reaching the celebrity gossip columns to the point where he became well known all over the world. His bold vision, his charisma, his unfettered ambition drew in investors, as moths to a flame. This is the insidious danger of such figures – Pied Pipers who lead the impressionable to part with their money. These figures have been around forever, but the phenomenon of the visionary founder, and the cult-like status that builds up around them, is a powerful but relatively new dynamic that has clouded the thinking of venture capitalists, dollar investors, and Wall Street itself, for the past 30 years.

Neumann is just one of a growing line of such figures. We will examine the Big Four – Jobs, Zuckerberg, Bezos and Musk – later in this book. Crash and burn certainly hasn't been their fate so far, but for the three still living, who knows? It certainly happened to Travis Kalanick at Uber; once similarly beguiling to investors as a visionary leader, he was forced out after evidence emerged of several incidents of inappropriate behaviour.

The problem for these businesses, as well as all their employees, suppliers, customers and communities, is that so much seems to rest on the personality of the leader. The reasons for their success are also their Achilles heel. Their originality of thinking, their brilliant ideas borne seemingly out of nowhere, their sparks of genius, their unique take on the world – all this is what helps to create the magic that leads to their success. The problem is that this isn't some Harvard Business School-style of business development. This is tear-up-the-rulebook, risk-taking, think big and bold entrepreneurship, often from characters whose backstory reads like a superhero origin movie. Troubled, driven, unpredictable, egotistical – combustible combinations which affect only immediate friends and family, until put in charge of corporations employing tens of thousands of people, propelled in a few short years to dizzying power and wealth. No wonder that sometimes the wheels come off in spectacular fashion.

A field of unicorns

Aileen Lee, is a venture capital investor and the founder of Cowboy Venture who, in 2013, coined the term 'unicorn' to describe a privately held start-up that achieves a value of over $1 billion. The unlikeliness of such a beast back then made it seem a highly appropriate term. In eight short years there are meadows full of grazing unicorns. There is even a 'Crunchbase Unicorn Leaderboard' that has, at the time of writing, 580 companies with a total valuation in excess of $2 trillion. How many of these have been founded by people who might be harbouring messianic missions in their hearts is hard to tell.

It is likely that most of these hundreds of unicorn tech companies have their genesis in a small back office and one or two great ideas, often thought up by a couple of enthusiastic geeks. Their propulsion to $1 billion valuation must, by definition, be swift, given that unicorns have only been around for a few years in this world. In those circumstances, is it surprising that individuals such as Neumann and Kalanick emerge, then crash and burn? It's probably more surprising that there aren't more of them. Or maybe there are, but they just don't have significant exposure beyond the Silicon Valley business press.

The continuing rise of unicorns and the writing-off of the Neumanns and Kalanicks as merely rogue one-offs means that the combustible, hothouse circumstances in which the charismatic yet ultimately hubristic leader can emerge and wreak havoc are still very much with us. The investor sector continues to chase the Next Big Thing, driven by FOMO – the fear of missing out. There will be more Neumanns and in Part 2 of this book we'll explore ways in which the risk of this can be minimized.

A house of cards

So, what was the WeWork endgame? The WeWork house of cards collapsed soon after the IPO announcement and 80 per cent of the stock has been bought by SoftBank, its largest investor, which has taken a $4.6 billion hit in the process. Neumann stepped down as CEO but still has limited ties to the business; in addition, he walked away from the wreckage with a cool $1.7 billion pay-out. Rebekah Neumann had various roles and interests in the We group but has now also stepped away from the business. In fact, the whole inner circle of around 20 people, all close friends of Neumann, who constituted what was referred to as Neumann's 'oval office', have all now left WeWork. Surrounding yourself in that way with a team – which will only ever answer 'yes' or 'how high?' to the instruction 'jump' – is another warning sign that hubris may have taken over.

Unsurprisingly, a young, charismatic and visionary co-founder can still travel a long way on chutzpah and a canny use of stock voting structures. The benefits of hindsight in the case of We are the same seemingly as so many other examples in the past. Shine too brightly too fast and there is a crash down to earth; gravity will always catch up with Icarus.

The hubris of Neumann is a warning that might be heeded by some people, but probably only briefly and until the next dazzling individual comes along to empty investors' pockets.

Tale 2: General Motors

General Motors (GM) was, and currently still is (despite some massive setbacks over the last few years) one of the giants of the US economy, employing approximately 180,000 people worldwide. During its 110+ year history, GM has embodied many of the guiding characteristics of successful US entrepreneurialism: aggressive expansion, thinking big, restlessly innovating and clever marketing. Way back in the 1920s GM came up with the very annoying yet highly effective marketing device of implementing small changes to the styling of models every year to make the previous year's model seem dated; something which has been causing needless envy among its rival manufacturers for over 100 years. The scale of GM's R&D resource was the stuff of legend and its investment has paid off over the years, with GM achieving some notable firsts in the automotive industry: in 1939, introducing the world's first automatic transmission system in a car, the Hydra-matic; in 1962, the first turbocharged engine in a car; and in 1972 the first rear-wheel anti-lock braking system. These are just three standout innovations from a vast list of firsts for GM.

As a large, complex business, GM developed organizational principles that changed forever how corporations around the US, and even the world, operated. In 1955 they became the first company to earn $1 billion a year. By 1962, GM had surpassed Ford in size and its US sales accounted for just over 50 per cent of all car sales, a staggering level of market domination. At the time, the president of GM, Charlie Wilson, summed up their position, saying, 'What's good for General Motors is good for America'. When you start making, and in turn believing, such statements, you know that a sense of proportion is slipping away. And so, from there, the only way was down. So when did signs of overreach, overconfidence and, yes, hubris, emerge at GM, culminating in their 2009 filing for bankruptcy? The roots of GM's fall from grace go back to the 1970s. The reason, suggests Aileen Lee, was – along with foreign competition, union battles, mismanagement and a failure to give consumers what they really wanted – hubris.

Despite the automotive industry changing rapidly, General Motors' executives did not deviate from their traditional formula for success. This lazy commitment to the mantra 'We have always done it this way' continued, even in the face of fast-shifting consumer trends and a succession of oil price shocks. General Motors' rigid adherence to its existing formula resulted in its market share dropping from 49 to 28 per cent within two decades.

The most common answer to why General Motors foundered is 'because it failed to make a profit'.

Peter Cohan, a writer for *Forbes* magazine, summed up why they failed to make a profit, saying simply what we already know: 'General Motors failed to innovate.' The firm did not really care about improving the quality of their vehicles or investing in new features; instead, the focus was on continuing to produce existing models that seemed to be the ones in demand by consumers, because at that point they were selling ... until they weren't. The focus was on quantity, not quality. In some ways, the conservatism of the US automotive market lulled GM into a false sense of security. Low taxation on gasoline (certainly when compared to Europe) ensured that fuel efficiency remained an insignificant consideration to the average US buyer, a situation that is still relatively true to this day – hence the continued popularity of SUVs. In that context, large, lumbering family cars continued to roll off the production line. GM's management failed to adapt, and their collective hubris as a company put them on the fast track to bankruptcy. Even something as drastic as a government bailout was unable to save them from their fate in 2009.

When Japanese auto manufacturers began to make cars that were better, more efficient and more reliable, General Motors simply couldn't keep up. Japanese manufacturers such as Toyota came up with leaner, more team-driven manufacturing processes which GM largely failed to understand and adopt.

Intriguingly, though, this is not a straight-line story. Even within GM there were pockets of enlightenment, which, for whatever reason, were not broadly adopted, even when success was demonstrated.

The GM and Toyota collaboration
One of the GM plants with a particularly chequered history was in Fremont, California. Established in 1962, it manufactured the Chevrolet Malibu, Buick Century and GMC trucks. Appalling industrial relations

and absenteeism running at 20 per cent per annum led to the plant's closure in 1982, an all-too-common occurrence for similar reasons across the US at that time. That is not, however, the end of the story. In 1983, the plant reopened, this time as a joint venture between GM and Toyota, under the name New United Motor Manufacturing, Inc. (NUMMI). Under the terms of this new arrangement, Toyota was responsible for running the plant, employing Japanese-style management. Team working, a revolutionary concept back then, was put in place, and had a transformative effect on industrial relations, in a plant where many of the same workforce was rehired and there was a legacy of resentment, antagonism and demarcation. At the plant when it had been GM, there had been no fewer than 100 different job classifications; in the new set-up, this was slashed to just four. Many different positive factors came into play as part of the plant's transformation, but the net effect was a massive increase in productivity, in quality performance and a transformation in working relationships. Pride and motivation were restored to new levels, ultimately resulting in Fremont, once the worst performing GM plant in the US, becoming the best.

General Motors previously had vast numbers of loyal buyers but lost them through what Micheline Maynard of the *New York Times* called 'A series of strategic and cultural missteps starting in the 1960s.' GM's fall from being the most powerful corporation in America to becoming the embodiment of failure, arrogance and hubris has been well documented. The saddest part of the GM story is that things could have been different. It didn't need to destroy thousands of lives by laying off thousands of workers. Had someone been able to step in and wrest control of the company, reversing the 'good ole boy' hubris, America's auto-manufacturing future could have been very different. This isn't a story about 'failure to make a profit'. It is a story of pride and arrogance and the power of hubris to destroy everything and everyone it touches.

In this regard, Maynard wrote, '[General Motors] bungled efforts in the 1980s to cut costs by sharing the underpinnings of its cars across different brands, blurring their distinctiveness. General Motors gave in to union demands in 1990 and created a program that paid workers even when plants were not running, forcing it to build cars and trucks [that] it could not sell without big incentives.'

That beacon of hope and common sense developed in conjunction with Toyota in Fremont, California, appears to have been a one-off, despite its obvious success. Instead of expanding this alliance and putting into practice the lessons learned, they appear to have remained in this pocket of the West Coast.

The EV1: the future isn't electric

Another nearly catastrophic moment for GM, and one of the most bizarre episodes in the company's recent history, is the story of the EV1 electric car, all of which is documented in a highly entertaining 2006 documentary, *Who Killed the Electric Car?*. This film explores the roles of GM, the oil industry, government and consumers in prematurely killing off one of the earliest commercializations of electric vehicles. For our purposes we will outline only GM's role, which was arrogant and contrary, to say the least.

The EV1 was, for its day in the mid-1990s, quite a futuristic looking car, and represents another 'first' from GM. It was the first purpose-designed, mass-produced electric vehicle to be manufactured by a major automotive company, pre-dating the Tesla Roadster by more than a decade. GM must surely look back to that time as one of their greatest 'if only' moments.

To make such reflection even more painful, the circumstances of the demise of the EV1 represent wilful self-destruction of the project. The EV1, from its launch in 1996 to its discontinuation in 2002, was only ever leased to owners rather than sold to them, in limited geographic zones of the US, principally Southern California. Customer reaction to the car was positive, in spite of its limited range as a result of battery technology at the time.

However, GM took the decision not only to discontinue production in 2002, but also to forcibly repossess the vehicles and destroy them. As a result, today the EV1 is even more rare and exotic than the futuristic DeLorean from several decades earlier.

The wheels fall off the Wagon(er)

As a case in point relating to hubristic behaviour, let's consider the contribution to GM of Rick Wagoner, CEO from 2000 until his resignation, at the insistence of the White House no less, on 29 March 2009. Wagoner had joined GM straight from Harvard in the late 1970s. He rose through the ranks, becoming COO in 1998 and then president and CEO two years later. He was elected chairman in 2003. Then, under his leadership, to top even the staggering haemorrhaging of cash GM had managed in the 1990s ($30 billion in a three-year period), under Wagoner's tenure the company lost more than $85 billion.

Plants were closed, production was slashed, but all these measures were insufficient in the face of decades of lack of direction and complacent management. Prior to succumbing to bankruptcy, Wagoner asked for support from the US government in the dog days of the Bush administration, just prior to Obama being elected president.

This was a moment of crisis right across the US automotive industry; not only was GM in trouble, so too were Ford and Chrysler. Consequently, the CEOs of this Big Three all sought support from the US government. In a you-couldn't-make-it-up moment of hubristic behaviour, Wagoner and the other two CEOs, for their initial government meeting, each flew to Washington DC, cap in hand, in corporate jets. Failing to spot the ill-judged symbolism of this, Wagoner declared, 'bankruptcy isn't an option'.

Things were finally taken out of Wagoner's hands, with incoming President Obama and Congress demanding that he step down as one of the conditions for GM receiving a significant portion of a $15 billion government support package to the US automotive industry. And so that 29 March 2009 resignation day arrived. However, just as in the Boeing story, tears didn't need to be shed for the departing CEO. Wagoner received an exit package worth in excess of $10 million.

The government's support package ended up failing, with both GM and Chrysler entering bankruptcy soon afterwards; Chrysler ended up merging with Fiat as part of its rescue plan.

Lessons still not learned: the ignition switch recall

As GM emerged from bankruptcy in 2010, a new management team took over and a significant amount of restructuring and reorganizing took place. Did this mean that old attitudes and practices had been consigned to history? Unfortunately, not quite. The most striking example of this was GM's handling of a vehicle recall, triggered by specific safety concerns relating to the ignition switch. As with the Boeing story, it is not so much the fault as the handling of that fault and attempts to cover it up that also, in this case, led to tragic consequences.

It is another story of cover-up, denial and fear of the cost of failure. The prevailing corporate culture in parts of GM must have been of such a nature that engineers at GM and lawyers representing the company chose to keep quiet for many years, even when well aware of a dangerous fault.

The ignition switch component in a number of GM vehicles was vulnerable to malfunction, which resulted in wildly unpredictable driving situations and has been linked to 124 deaths. GM was aware of this issue as far back as 2005. It also ordered half a million replacement ignition switches nearly two months before making its first recall, which only occurred nearly 10 years on, in 2014. Millions of vehicles were eventually recalled at a cost of billions of dollars, plus a string of lawsuits and compensation payments. What was deemed to be costly and time-consuming to fix at the outset, via millions of vehicles recalled, ended up, yet again, costing far more in the long term.

GM's reputation, in the face of tragic and avoidable deaths, was critically damaged. Although there is no evidence that the new C-suite team at GM after 2010, including CEO Mary Barra, had any knowledge of this issue prior to the recall process finally taking place, there was clearly still a culture in place, pre- and post-bankruptcy, where arrogance, as well as an above-the-law and above-the-regulator attitude, was prevalent in some crucial parts of the business. Again, there are echoes of the attitude crisis at Boeing, particularly in relation to industry regulators.

As an example, however enlightened and forward-looking the public face of the organization (and GM's first female CEO and her team have transformed the perception of the business; see below), if there is a cancer of arrogance, self-interest, secrecy and the preservation of profit at the expense of all other considerations, in short a fatal pride, then cover-ups with potentially fatal consequences will continue to occur.

Boeing and GM share some common aspects: they are both involved in manufacturing and marketing products where faults can have fatal consequences. Thankfully this wasn't the case with WeWork. As dominant market leaders in their sectors, both GM and Boeing have displayed behaviour that suggests they see themselves as too big to need to be governed by external forces. However, as the history of commerce over the past 100 years has shown, ultimately no business is too big to fail.

GM renaissance?

Aside from the recall issue and a few other bumps in the road for GM in the past decade, is there now a new, less proud attitude at play? Certainly, the performance and stance from GM's first-ever female CEO (and first female CEO to lead a global automotive business) Mary Barra, who has been in post since 2014, is encouraging. Indeed, GM has gone further in its gender trailblazing, with its CFO also a woman, Dhivya Suryadevara – again a first ever 'one-two' of that nature in the automotive industry.

Does female influence dissipate and diffuse hubris? If that is too broad a question to be posited as a universal truth, Barra and her team certainly appear to be adopting a more customer-focused, receptive stance in relation to the future of the automotive industry, and they are placing far less emphasis on past glories and old attitudes.

The future is electric

After the farcical EV1 episode in the 1990s, GM has lost the best part of 20 years of initiative in developing all-electric vehicles, allowing Tesla to ride up on the inside rail and place itself in a prime position ahead of GM. By early 2020, Tesla's stock was worth more than the combined value of GM and Ford. That is a staggering change in fortune in such a short time (see Chapter 4 for further insights on Musk and Tesla).

The success of electric vehicles depends on battery technology, something that Tesla recognized from the outset. Finally at GM, that realization seems to have occurred, too. While GM has been manufacturing electric cars under its Volt brand since the mid/late 2000s, it was only in 2019 that GM struck a major alliance with one of the world's largest battery manufacturers, South Korea's LG Chem. Will this be enough to unlock the true potential at GM for it even to begin the fightback against Tesla? Time will tell.

It is in market situations like these that there is a potential and critical hairline distinction in attitude that makes all the difference. A swift and deft transition – of the kind that is now required from a reliance on the internal combustion engine to electric power – is pivotal for the entire automotive industry, and it's a transition that will require boldness, decisiveness and swift action. In the right hands those are all virtues, both in entrepreneurial terms and in attitude. In the wrong hands, however, boldness can become arrogance, decisiveness can become dictatorial behaviour, and swiftness can become a steamrollering approach, all with just a small change of emphasis.

Do Barra and her team at GM have the right balance to make things happen, keep the business in the game and yet avoid the legacy of hubris that seems so deeply ingrained at GM? Right now, no one knows, but one thing is for sure – the battle royale between Tesla and GM (and the rest) is going to be one of the most fascinating business stories of the 2020s.

Tale 3: Uber

This is an instructive story about how a corporate culture, borne out of the arrogance of senior executives, cheapened and undermined the reputation and possible long term success of a business founded on a great idea.

Co-founder and former CEO Travis Kalanick oversaw incredible growth at Uber, all set against a background of multiple accusations of sexual harassment and unethical competitive practices at the company during his reign. From the top down, an air of invincibility and arrogance continues to haunt Uber.

Chancer Travis

Travis Kalanick acknowledges that the basic genius ride share/ride hail idea of Uber wasn't his, but he was the figure who powered its move, in eight tumultuous years between 2009 and 2017, from great idea to innovation phenomenon. Kalanick became involved with Uber at the age of 33, after already having led a colourful business life in his twenties. His first business, Scour Inc., included a peer-to-peer file-sharing service, which attracted a multi-billion-dollar lawsuit from the US music and movie industries alleging copyright infringement.

Seemingly uncowed by this, his second venture, Red Swoosh, was also a peer-to-peer file-sharing venture. This time a run-in with the IRS brought things to a grinding halt. With these past ventures on his CV, he then became involved with the nascent Uber, brought in as an adviser to the team that first developed the Uber concept, including the man with the original idea, Garrett Camp.

Disruptor Uber

The dizzying rise of Uber and its hubristic ride straight through and past competitors, law enforcement agencies and regulators is so astonishingly brazen that it continues to raise serious questions about the seeming powerlessness and ineffectiveness of any levers of corporate restraint. Uber appears to have moved from maverick local operator to a global force seemingly too big to halt or restrain within such a short time period that every stakeholder, competitor or regulator has been left floundering in its wake. Uber came to personify the worst possible example of a taxi ride: dirty, careless of the rules of the road, rude, argumentative, unreliable and ultimately leaving you stranded where you didn't want to be.

Accusations against Uber's practices fall into two categories: admitted failings and misdemeanours; and those things that up until the recent court ruling it was still trying to defend but which are subject to a huge array of challenges and disputes. To illustrate Uber's above-the-law stance, here are some examples.

Failings Uber has admitted to:

- misleading drivers about their potential earnings;
- underpaying New York City drivers by millions of dollars;
- requesting rides with competitors, only to cancel them;
- developing and using software to avoid giving rides to law enforcement officers in areas where its service was illegal;
- lax data security procedures, resulting in several hacks into personal data held by Uber;
- inadequate background checking and vetting of drivers.

Alleged failings which Uber disputes:

- cynical price hikes during emergencies such as during the UK June 2017 London Bridge attack;
- continued classification of drivers as contractors rather than employees: this is the biggest issue surrounding the terms and conditions for Uber drivers and the dispute rumbles on;
- anti-trust price fixing;
- a pattern of highly aggressive strategies against competitors and regulators.

Online you can find many more accusations and examples of aggressive, arrogant practices by Uber in its short corporate life so far. Except in the US and Canada, where Lyft is a significant competitor to Uber, it continues to have a virtual monopoly in its sector, never a healthy position for any business when viewed from the perspective of retaining a sense of responsibility and restraint.

Bullying and harassment

It is perhaps not surprising that, on top of bullying and harassment of competitors and regulators, came internal accusations of bullying and harassment of staff. A corporate culture and business practices which appear not just to tolerate but to revel in aggression, arrogance and a feeling of invincibility in its trading stance is one where the internal culture can all too easily mirror that.

Accusations that in 2017 Kalanick was aware of allegations of sexual harassment but chose to do nothing have become extremely well known. A number of other similar accusations have subsequently emerged, culminating in Kalanick stepping down as CEO of Uber in June 2017. To complete our trio of 'Don't feel too bad for them' departing executives, Kalanick's net worth is still listed in *Forbes* magazine as being in excess of $3 billion.

Uber Uber

Does the name of a business influence its culture? 'Uber' as an adjective adds extremity to any word that it prefixes, and it's had particular resonance in the last 10 years – i.e. since Uber has been around. Uber, the company, is not just aggressive, it is *uber* aggressive. It has been 'very' at everything, with firepower in the form of expensive crack legal teams to fight off local, regional, national and even international jurisdictions from curbing its business.

Uber's model was built on the belief that it was beyond the reach of legislative action or rules, and on the belief that it had it torn up the rulebook on employee status and employee protection. It could be argued that Uber is one of the principal drivers (literally in their case) of the rise of the gig economy, that chimera of employee flexibility and control, except for the fact that millions of workers around the world became trapped in Uber's model.

Uber's future

The simple genius of its original idea is so strong that, along with such a powerful first mover advantage, it looks like keeping Uber in a dominant position for the foreseeable future. Canny acquisitions of related services and logical diversification into areas such as food delivery look set to keep it ahead of any possible competitors. In a fractured, diffused worker economy, the Uber opportunity looks to be one to which millions will continue to sign up.

What does it all say about our culture?

As a signifier of prevailing business culture, there is, frankly, something depressing about what Uber represents. There is a strange dichotomy surrounding it. Beloved by millennials, its app-based instant gratification (with one click your ride is minutes away) makes the bus, the subway or the traditional taxi seem like conformist, old-school modes of transport. With its ride-share option, surely there is something co-operative and even communitarian in its ethos?

Well, yes, a bit … but largely no. Once upon a time, the community was every town and city's taxi drivers sharing their taxi ranks, each a font of local knowledge and not just the A–Z street map. With Uber, each driver looks out for themselves, seeking to oust all other forms of transport rather than work alongside them on the shared understanding that a transport system is an interrelated network. This may seem like nothing more than misty-eyed nostalgia for a creaking transport model ripe for replacement and a good shake-up. However, there is a 'race to the bottom' feel about the Uber model, which in the short term may benefit the consumer, but in the long term has the potential to hollow out every city's transport ecosystem to a point where, quite suddenly, choice and flexibility no longer exist.

The brutal individualism of the Uber model, and the reflection of that in the occasional glimpses of its corporate culture, are not encouraging signifiers of a dissipation of what could be regarded as a hubristic culture. Uber-aggression, uber-individualism, uber exploitation are all hallmarks of a business culture and even a society which is inward-looking, selfish and anti-co-operative.

Tale 4: Deutsche Bank

Deutsche Bank's expansion in the 1990s led to it becoming the biggest bank in the world, with assets in excess of $2 trillion. However, its power and aggressive culture led to widespread money laundering and market manipulation, to the point where this once-revered institution is now considered an exemplar of corporate hubris.

In 2020, Deutsche Bank (DB) celebrated its 150th anniversary, a significant landmark for most organizations of its size. There has been some celebration, of course, but this activity is somewhat muted, perhaps because from 2016 onwards the shareholder dividend has wavered between zero and under 0.2 per cent. In the same period, its net income has only once briefly stepped into the black but otherwise has been firmly in the red. Of course, all major global financial institutions have been dealing with the massive aftershocks of the 2008 financial crisis and Deutsche Bank is not alone in taking a considerable amount of time to recover from this. However, its pattern of behaviour since 2008 seems to indicate that it has failed to learn the lessons of that crisis and has indeed doubled down on its risk-taking and in egregious corporate behaviour.

We cannot attempt here a detailed dissection of the strategic financial reasons that have led to the bank's current parlous standing in the world of banking. Of more interest, perhaps, is a glimpse into its culture and therefore the sanctioned attitude towards risk and transparency. Such attitudes in the financial sector are hardly restricted to Deutsche Bank alone. They show a loss of connection between the bank's financial manoeuvrings and the people whose lives are affected, often shattered, by their outcomes. In common with many other banks and financial institutions, huge paper financial moves became merely numbers on a balance sheet rather than key transactions affecting the lives of millions. This abstraction led the sector to a shared, often consensual, blindness, that all these actions were just clever playing of the market and thus merely victimless crimes.

This slipping of the moorings of understanding the reality of the cause and effect of their actions created an addiction to it all as a high-stakes game, an adrenalin-rush gamble, with huge wins to be made through manipulation and clever out-thinking of the market. This created a moral vacuum, which bred, from the top down, a feeling of invincibility, of a perceived refined level of understanding of what they were doing being above that of anyone outside their world. *This is all so clever and sophisticated and fast-moving that to be transparent about it all ... well, you just wouldn't understand the nuance and cleverness of it.*

Brand lustre

Deutsche Bank is coated in a glossy veneer of corporate probity, as glittering as the reflective glass in its twin-tower headquarters in Frankfurt. Indeed, to the man in the street there is a gravitas and heft bestowed upon it by its name alone: Deutsche Bank. Maybe this contributed to it being able to operate like some wolf in sheep's clothing for so long. In most sectors, a German brand name signifies quality, precision, design and modernity. The top 10 most valuable German brands in 2019 were, in descending order, SAP, Deutsche Telekom, Mercedes-Benz, BMW, Adidas, DHL, Aldi, Siemens, Bosch and Allianz. What other country or economy can boast such an impressive shortlist? DB is not part of that list but its 'Deutsche' has benefited from the post-war halo effect that its German counterparts have helped to bestow upon it. If it is *Deutsche*, then it must be sensible and dependable, even stolid and cautious; probably forward-looking, clever and resourceful, too.

To examine the chequered history of DB over the last 20 years creates a cognitive dissonance when considering the various activities and scandals it has been embroiled in. What? *Deutsche Bank*?!

Deutsche Bank continues on as Deutsche Bank, with few signs of that changing. The reaction to the various failings has been, to the outside world, little more than a shrug. How else could it, even now, continue to be the largest banking institution in Germany, Europe's largest economy?

Too big to fail

Deutsche Bank is part of an alarmingly long list of financial institutions considered too big to fail, and therefore requiring eye-watering bailouts from governments and central banks. In the context of hubris, the phrase 'too big to fail' is often synonymous. In one context it implies an understanding by the world's economies that there are financial institutions underpinning it which must, under all circumstances, be able to continue to function and enjoy the confidence of investors. The Dodd–Frank Wall Street Reform and Consumer Protection Act followed in 2010, introduced in the wake of the financial crisis, and to the labelling of such banks as 'systemically important financial institutions (SIFIs)', with DB included in that category. In other words, they continue to be too big to fail.

Another way of looking at that phrase is from an internal perspective: *we're* too big to fail. This starts to get to the heart of the matter – i.e., the root of the cultural failings within Deutsche Bank. 'We're too big to fail' is just a small step away from 'We just can't fail', the giddy confident statement of the speculator who is sure that they have found a scheme which is so ingenious yet so fool-proof that it is bound to succeed.

Deutsche Bank's controversies have resulted in fines totalling in excess of $15 billion (although, shockingly, Citigroup, JPMorgan Chase and Bank of America have all exceeded Deutsche Bank in their levels of fines since the financial crash). On that basis, the moral relativism at play in the financial sector has been so skewed that, in that company, Deutsche Bank must have thought it was playing by a set of parallel rules to those of common decency and honesty.

The Big Short

We used a documentary film, *Who Killed the Electric Car?*, as a reference point in the General Motors tale, and another movie (and book), *The Big Short*, makes a great reference point in relation to Deutsche Bank.

It focuses on Greg Lippmann, head of global CDO (collateralized debt obligation) in the period leading up to the 2008 financial crash. The whole caper becomes fiendishly complicated but, to quote Bloomberg, Lippmann 'offset losses on mortgage investments with wagers against subprime debt that made $1.5 billion'.

We have singled out Lippmann and CDO trading among the litany of Deutsche Bank goings-on because of the closed loop nature of the incident. It is clear that two parts of the bank were making money from mutually opposite activity. During the housing credit bubble of 2004/08, at the same time that Lippmann was making money by betting that the CDO market value would fall dramatically (which it duly did), other divisions of DB were continuing to pull in investors in these financial products. They made money, too, so both parties won ... for a while. Of course, such a strategy cannot, by definition, produce winning results for everyone in the long term, as Deutsche Bank would have been fully aware. As an example of overbearing arrogance, it is hard to beat. Deutsche Bank, knowing it was Too Big to Fail, felt that the risk of this high-wire act was therefore worth taking. The buck to be made was a stronger pull than the threat of the buck that would stop with the bank. But alas, despite the significant turmoil caused, banks have since begun to sell billions in CDOs, seemingly learning nothing from history.

Banking hubris

So, in the light of that coda to *The Big Short*, is hubris in banking both institutional and ingrained? An inability or a downright unwillingness to learn from mistakes would appear to be a recurring trait and that surely is a characteristic of hubris. Seemingly the fastest growing part of the financial sector since the financial crash has been the number and size of fines, which have racked up a staggering $243 billion in the 10 years between 2008 and 2018. Faced with these monumental sums, have the banks been investing in systemic remedies to the culture and practices of their businesses? The signs aren't promising. There has been a pattern across the banking sector of an acceleration in returning money to shareholders in the form of stock buy-backs and dividends (even if at DB the results have been so dire that dividends have simply not been possible in recent times).

Later in this book we will be exploring ways in which these stubborn cultural hubristic tendencies can be tackled. Depressingly, as their practices and behaviour materially affect the lives of all of us and not just the 'markets', the banking sector remains one of the most challenging in terms of finding ways to dismantle its inherent arrogance, borne out of Too Big to Fail being seen as a rallying cry rather than the warning sign it actually represents.

CHAPTER 4

Walking the Hubris Tightrope

Too proud to lead?

The high-profile, buccaneering CEO, with vision and drive, continues to be a model to be looked up to. This is partly due to the efforts of a handful of people who have become household names, transcending their industries and achieving superstar status. Jobs, Zuckerberg, Bezos and Musk – their careers have affected multiple aspects of all our lives. Their wealth, power and influence are dizzying, far more so than those of any previous generations of entrepreneurs. Has their success been achieved by avoiding hubris through channelling the upsides of determination, ambition, drive and vision?

Case study 1: Steve Jobs

The flawed genius of Steve Jobs as designer, inventor and visionary led Apple to become, for a time, the most valuable company in the world. His life and career have been the subject of numerous books and movies, but here we take a sideways look at Jobs from a perspective of assessing him and his legacy via its hubristic tendencies.

'Steve Jobs hubris'

Google 'Steve Jobs' and you will find a plethora of articles, opinion pieces and examples of Steve Jobs the genius. Pay closer attention to what those who knew him well thought of him, or examine some of his actions and decisions, and you start to see references to hubristic tendencies. Interestingly, it is around the 18 months leading up to his early death in October 2011 at the age of 56 that references to hubris seem to increase. During this period, as his illness took hold and he was forced to take leave of absence, while still remaining CEO, investors and commentators started to take stock and evaluated whether Apple was solely dependent on Jobs and what its future would be if he was no longer around.

In March 2010, Jeff McMahon, posting as 'herculodge', wrote this under the headline, 'Is Steve Jobs Driven by Hubris?'

'Today Leo Laporte said on his tech show on KFI that Steve Jobs doesn't make Apple products to please customers. He makes them as he wants them and, contrary to any other company, he does not even do consumer testing to see what their appeal may or not be. So, if you'd like certain things improved on your Apple products, forget about it. Do it Steve Jobs' way. Is this the ultimate in hubris or what?'

While it would be easy to jump on the hubris bandwagon, the counter-argument to 'doing things the Steve Jobs way', is, of course, his track record of success. By 2010/11, from a perspective of 10 years, Steve Jobs had every right to trust his instincts and his own judgement. After all, it is hard to think of many individuals who, in the past 50 years, have hit a home run as impressive as Macintosh computer, iMac, iTunes, iPod, iPhone, iPad, plus let's add in Pixar and effectively creating mass-market access to desktop publishing, plus many other innovations. It's no exaggeration to say that Steve Jobs changed the way the world works. So we should be careful to distinguish between outright success, to be admired and applauded, and hubris. In 2010/11, however, it was easy to get the jitters on Apple's behalf about Jobs' desire to maintain a vice-like grip on all key decisions in the business.

The above quote by McMahon, which reads like a lament in 2010, was at the heart of Jobs' strength and power in the decade leading up to that point. While other companies invested time and effort in focus groups and testing, Jobs, in partnership with his genius designer, the Englishman Jonathan Ive, produced that home run of astonishing products based almost entirely on his own powerful vision on what he believed people wanted; there are an astonishing 450+ product patents registered in Jobs' name. He recognized that, in the field of consumer electronics, people don't know what they want until you show it to them. And that by running with a particular 'less is more' design aesthetic, you could add an aura of cool to almost anything. He recognized early on that, of course, the most difficult audience to impress with a design is designers. But that as a set of opinion-formers, if you could get them using, promoting and ultimately fervently evangelizing your products, you had a cult that could become a movement, and which in time could become a mass religion.

The deification of Steve

Apple became, rather uncomfortably, a creed, a belief, almost akin to a religion. Whether Jobs himself was comfortable with that is hard to gauge but he didn't seem to actively dissuade people from moving in that direction. His ascetic adopted uniform of an Issey Miyake black turtleneck sweater, blue jeans and sneakers reinforced the 'less is more' mantra. The logo, store layouts, advertising, packaging, HQ design and, of course, the products themselves, to believers took on the importance of religious relics as well as being products that improved users' productivity and their enjoyment of life.

And so, like most organized religions, if you are not a believer, then you must be its opposite – an unbeliever. And lo, Jobs did cast the unbelievers into the wilderness. Bill Gates, Michael Dell, Larry Page and Sergey Brin were all seemingly unbelievers, along with whoever represented Adobe and countless other non-Apple players in technology in the 90s and early 2000s.

The walled garden

It also came to pass that Jobs did create a garden in which there was an apple tree. This was not the garden of Eden, but a walled garden for Apple and its disciples to live and work in. In this walled garden, the serpent of knowledge, of outside knowledge, was banished. Taking a bite out of the apple not only created Apple's logo, but it also bestowed a world of Apple knowledge upon its believers. Work and play and music and communication were all available in a way not seen before.

It is here, in this walled garden, that Jobs' hubris is finally laid bare. It was not enough for him to create cool, innovative, beautifully designed products. That's what any number of entrepreneurs have done over the past 100 years. Jobs wanted to create an entire lifestyle, a way of living and working that was, via an Apple interface, available 24/7. In 2010, when comparing the emerging Android strategy from Google with Apple's approach, Jobs said, 'We think [Google's] open versus closed argument is just a smokescreen to try and hide the real issue, which is, "What's best for the customer?"' There it is again: Jobs' view that it is, in fact, he who knows what is best for the customer. A belief in his own self-importance, validated on the basis of a string of successes, sheds light on how confidence and success can easily start to morph into hubris.

Life in the walled garden has continued in the decade since Jobs' death, with the number of believers living and working in it continuing to grow, to levels, in fact, that even Jobs may never have dared to hope. Apple's net income was $14 billion in 2010; Apple's revenue for the 12-month period to September 2020 was almost $275 billion. Its market capitalization mushroomed over the same period and, famously, in April 2018 Apple became the world's first trillion-dollar company. It has since comfortably exceeded that figure, making it larger than the GDP of many substantial sized nations such as Mexico, Indonesia and the Netherlands.

The Cook era

Under Tim Cook's stewardship, Apple has carefully and rather cautiously milked the design and innovation legacy that Jobs bestowed on Apple. Considered 10 years on, while lamenting Jobs' departure, whether by luck or judgement, in Tim Cook Apple found what could be argued was the perfect successor … for a while. We will come to that important caveat shortly, as it addresses the true hubris surrounding Jobs, which is only now fully revealing itself.

Jobs innovated, Cook sells. That, in a nutshell, is the stark difference in approach and outlook between the two men. If Jobs was the maître d', then Cook is, well, in a piece of nominative determinism … the cook. Jobs was front-of-house, inspiring customers as they came in, delighting everyone with the innovative, unique and original dishes he kept adding to the Apple menu. Cook is labouring in the kitchen, occasionally appearing in the restaurant to make an announcement, but basically still relying on the menu that the maître d' dreamed up a decade ago. And there are signs that the customers are getting bored with the same food over and over again. The restaurant's decor has aged remarkably well, as grey minimalist cool is hardly likely to go out of fashion, but the entrées are still basically the same, with just a few changes to the garnish on the side. However, the restaurant is keeping busy, flourishing even, when many other establishments have closed down or merged with others to create bland chain restaurants.

Apple's days as an innovator and an exciting trendsetter have slowly disappeared. This is perhaps inevitable, as each market it operates in has moved from growth to maturity, from quantum leaps in innovation to inching-forward iterations. The days when the launch day of the latest version of the iPhone had people sleeping on the streets outside Apple stores, to be the first in the queue when the doors opened, are long gone. The whole world now has a smartphone, and even budget iPhone lookalike models have more features than most of their users know what to do with. The phone is now our computer, music player, sophisticated camera and personal assistant all in one handy, easy to take for granted device. New model with an extra camera lens and a bevelled screen? Meh.

The fall of the wall

It came to pass that the Apple followers started to look over the wall of the garden and began to question why the wall was there at all. And so, there will come a moment, inevitably, when the Apple wall will fall. We can't predict when this will happen, but if the history of commerce teaches us anything, it will happen at some point. The Apple wall has survived for close to 10 years, since Jobs' death in 2011, but can it survive for another 10 or 20? Or will it cease to have a purpose? Whenever it occurs, it will be at that moment that Steve Jobs' vision for Apple will be exposed as being hubristic and proud. Certainly, the wall has already been breached in places, with Siri working with Amazon devices, and with Spotify sitting alongside Apple Music on devices, and so on. But the entire unique ecosystem of special high-priced charging cables, operating systems and dedicated supply chain and retailers is still in place ... for now.

Pride before a fall

Until the dismantling of the walled garden, whenever that may occur, there is no denying that it will have been a good run. However, the faults in the very wall's foundations are ones of pride, overconfidence and, yes, hubris.

Open source

The contrast in approach is stark when you look at the philosophy behind the development of the operating systems of Apple and of Google's Android. In the introduction to the Android Open Source Project is this statement:

> 'Android is an *open source* operating system for mobile devices and a corresponding *open source* project led by Google. ... As an *open source* project, *Android's* goal is to avoid any central point of failure in which one industry player can restrict or control the innovations of any other player.'

This last, pointed comment is clearly aimed at Apple. Now, Google is not perhaps best placed to claim to be the unalloyed good guy in this argument between the two businesses. Steve Jobs famously called out the Google motto 'Don't be evil' as 'It's bullshit' and he may well have been right. But in relation to its decision to make Android open source, this is surely a more inclusive, pluralistic and democratic path than Apple's. It demonstrates a humility that within Google (or now parent company Alphabet) they don't hold all the ideas and all the development answers; that the hive mind is more effective in solving problems and connecting the needs and concerns of customers with workable solutions.

Apple's stance, by contrast, is Jobsian in its outlook; they are incredibly restrictive in terms of hardware and device maintenance. Further than that, because Apple's is a walled-off app store, there is no pesky free stuff being given away needlessly. Apple imposes a 30 per cent surcharge on all payments made through its app store. Spotify was so frustrated by this that it issued elaborate guidance to Apple users as to the best way to circumvent this if choosing to use Spotify on an Apple device. Similarly, while Spotify offers a free music listening app as an entry point (subsidized by advertising), Apple offers no such concession. Want Apple Music? Everyone but everyone pays.

Apple Genius Bar

Genius is an overused word. The dictionary defines it as 'A person of exceptional ability, esp. of a highly original kind'. Steve Jobs deserves that description, no question. The people in his stores who have a go at fixing your iPhone when it freezes … while amazingly helpful, not so much. There is a knowingness and even a playfulness to the branding of Apple's Genius Bar. But is it yet another tiny signifier of Apple's we-know-best hubristic attitude, the creation of a million setting-up-for-a-fall moments.

1984

As well as being a visionary with regard to tech products, Jobs was also a masterful marketeer. Apple's advertising has, from the outset, perfectly reflected its desired positioning: alternative, cool, designed, different. This approach exploded on to the world's TV screens in 1984 with the hammer blow at the end of Apple's iconic *1984* ad. Referencing Orwell's book of the same name, this Ridley Scott-directed one-minute advert was first screened at peak time during the third quarter of Super Bowl XVIII in January 1984. In a dystopian future, grey workers march along and then are seated watching Big Brother on a huge screen intone the latest official announcement:

'Today we celebrate the first glorious anniversary of the Information Purification Directives. We have created for the first time in all history a garden of pure ideology, where each worker may bloom, secure from the pests of any contradictory true thoughts. Our Unification of Thoughts is more powerful a weapon than any fleet or army on earth. We are one people, with one will, one resolve, one cause. Our enemies shall talk themselves to death and we will bury them with their own confusion. We shall prevail!' Burnham, David (4 March 1984). 'The Computer, the Consumer and Privacy'. *New York Times*, Washington DC.

Running up through this grey crowd is the vivid figure of a female athlete in a white singlet and red shorts who hurls a large hammer at the screen just as this speech ends, causing it to explode into white light. Up the screen then scrolls this text plus voiceover:

On January 24th,
Apple Computer will introduce
Macintosh.
And you'll see why 1984
won't be like '1984.'

Fade to black screen with the rainbow-coloured version of the Apple logo centre screen. Ad ends.

The hammer represented Apple smashing the then largest PC manufacturer, Big Blue itself, IBM and its dominant DOS operating system.

Fast-forward to 2010/11 and beyond and where had Jobs' hubris taken Apple? Far from being the plucky underdog, Apple became one of the sector's primary forces, long since consigning IBM and many others to the margins of the history books. It still paints itself as the edgy alternative, but wait, let's look again at part of Big Brother's speech:

> 'We have created for the first time **in all history a garden of pure ideology**, where each worker may bloom, secure from the pests of any contradictory true thoughts.'

Surely at this point one is reminded of the final lines of Orwell's other famous work, *Animal Farm*, where the distinctions between men and pigs have become blurred, and it is no longer possible to say which is which.

In less than 30 years, Apple had become the very thing it purported to despise in the ad: the suppressor of any contradictory true thoughts. Jobs' mission could be regarded as complete – the believers now believed unquestioningly.

Steve Jobs' hubris

More even than the other subjects of our case studies, Zuckerberg, Bezos and Musk, there is a totally inextricable binding up of the man and his work. Steve Jobs **was Apple**, and Apple **was Steve Jobs**. And it became a platform for him to evangelize his unique vision. The entire way in which the business became structured and went to market, from that *1984* ad onwards, reflected his outlook, his approach and his philosophy. One which brooked no argument or criticism, one where the cult of personality had coincided perfectly with dizzying excitement for the possibilities opened up by portable technology.

Hidden away from the utopian vision have been various inconvenient truths. Exploitative labour practices in China and elsewhere; products with obsolescence designed into them; a poor environmental record; along with other tech giants, a 'creative' approach to paying tax in local jurisdictions; some would argue also, overpriced products cushioned by an aura of cool and status … the list goes on.

As such, the dazzling life and career of Steve Jobs is instructive when doing one's best to guard against hubris and its effects. The cult of his personality, the force of his will and the strength of his vision were powerful tools that enabled him not only to make a comeback from being fired from Apple in 1985 to then come back in 1997 even stronger, but from there to go on to be *the* dominant figure in the tech and entertainment industry for the next decade.

But all this came at a price. Surrounding himself with acolytes and fans, *Jobs came to believe the legend instead of the reality.* Apple moved from being a business to becoming a cult, surely a status which always distorts and bends the facts. Whether it ends in triumph or disaster is yet to be known. What is undeniable, though, is that it remains probably the most fascinating business journey of the past 50 years and it is one in which the signs of hubristic tendencies of its co-founder, Steve Jobs, have played a pivotal role. From reviewing Jobs' career, it's clear that confidence, belief, boldness, vision, all matter when creating successful organizations. Yet what needs to be guarded against is when it becomes all-encompassing, and a leader fails to see the blind spots to which he/she has become oblivious.

Case study 2: Mark Zuckerberg

Zuckerberg's character has been picked over as much as that of Steve Jobs', particularly as Facebook is a business made in the image of its founder in a similar way to the relationship between Apple and Jobs. This is a man whose influence on the world, it may be argued, is the most far-reaching of all our case studies.

You may never have owned an Apple product, you may never buy from Amazon (OK, that one is unlikely) and the majority of us may not own a Tesla car. But 'never used Facebook' is a statement that can probably be truthfully stated by the smallest percentage of people reading this book. 'Never use Facebook' – note the use of the present tense here – now that would be a slightly bigger percentage, as fatigue, boredom and cynicism towards the Facebook platform have mounted over the past decade.

The reasons for the growth in cynicism towards Facebook is an increased questioning of its true motives, and here we will see parallels below in the current position of Amazon and Bezos, where its true purpose is coming under increased scrutiny. What marks out Facebook and Zuckerberg from Jobs/Apple, Bezos/Amazon and Musk/Tesla (and indeed our subjects in Chapter 3, WeWork, GM, Uber and Deutsche Bank) is that Facebook is free to use.

It's free!

Free to use, with all its amazing facilities and ability to connect us. It is in fact surprisingly easy to forget this and to take it for granted. Of course, Facebook is not unique in that regard, as nearly all social media platforms are free to users, as are so many amazingly useful apps. At the height of the Covid-19 lockdown, the immense value of the Zoom video meeting facility (and many other similar apps) in providing vital human and commercial connections has become clear. It could be argued that Zuckerberg and another handful of pioneers created the template for free and open communication and connection. Well, that is the utopian interpretation of what is going on. Yet, of course, Facebook *isn't* free. It's one of the most profitable companies in the world, funded by advertising that's powered by the most fiendishly clever set of algorithms on the planet.

It's all about data

It is this that makes Facebook not 'free' at all. We pay for it handsomely: with our data. And what riches in data we so freely give. 'Would you like to subscribe to our email newsletter?', offering a simple exchange of your name and your email address in return for some possibly useful information. Millions of companies rely on that simple bargain in order to develop some sort of relationship with us and wrest our precious email address from our jealously guarded control, along with our even more precious permission to send stuff to it. That is merely a skimming-the-surface approach for the likes of Facebook. Two pieces of data? Just name and email address? We freely give Facebook thousands of pieces of data about ourselves. It knows more about our lifestyle, our preferences, our opinions and our behaviour than some members of our family probably do. It knows who our friends and family are, where we go, the things we like … and the products and services we like to buy. It begs the question: is this an outrageous intrusion into every corner of our private lives? Yet, most of us are likely to shrug and keep revealing more of it to Zuckerberg. Why? Because it's giving us a voice and helping to bring us all together. At least, that is what Facebook has manoeuvred us into thinking.

In October 2019, Mark Zuckerberg made a speech at Georgetown University, and Facebook made available the transcript. Within it, he took the opportunity to reiterate exactly that higher purpose:

'I've focused on building services to do two things: give people voice and bring people together. These two simple ideas — voice and inclusion — go hand in hand.'

The bulk of the speech was devoted to this topic:

'I'm here today because I believe we must continue to stand for free expression.'

It is here that Zuckerberg was clearly on the defensive, with Facebook (and its sister platform Instagram) reeling from accusations of being a platform that enables the spread of hate speech and cyber-bullying, as well as having become the distorted mirror whereby so many people are informed about politics and current affairs (we will discuss this in more detail below). His libertarian defence of free speech is one that grapples with the genie that Facebook has let out of the bottle: creating millions, billions, of keyboard warriors able to spread anything they like into the echo chambers of their Friends.

Zuckerberg concluded his speech with this rousing slice of idealism:

> 'I believe in giving people a voice because, at the end of the day, I believe in people. And as long as enough of us keep fighting for this, I believe that more people's voices will eventually help us work through these issues together and write a new chapter in our history – where from all of our individual voices and perspectives, we can bring the world closer together.'

Just as with the 'free' bit, this takes some reminding, too. He is still only in his thirties. And he runs a company, not society at large. If we need reminding, then so it seems does Zuckerberg himself. His hubristic ambitions now show few bounds.

The Social Network

Let's go back to the beginnings of Facebook and again back to the movies. Has there ever been a better movie about an American business and its origins than *The Social Network*? Beautifully directed by David Fincher, incisively written by Aaron Sorkin and wonderfully played by the whole cast, released in 2010 it remains a must-see movie. Interestingly, Sorkin, when asked about his reasons for getting involved, said,

> 'What attracted me to [the film project] had nothing to do with Facebook. The invention itself is as modern as it gets, but the story is as old as storytelling; the themes of friendship, loyalty, jealousy, class and power.'

It is this last one, power, that leaves the lasting impression from the story as it is told in the film. Above all other considerations, you are left with the feeling that it is power that the young Zuckerberg craves above everything else. The warm words at the end of that 2019 speech do their best to disguise a coldness of purpose and ultimately a potentially at-odds, basic hypocrisy, at the heart of Facebook.

What started out as a simple impulse to look cleverer than the other frat boys in his year at college has somehow morphed crazily into a platform for Zuckerberg to claim he's setting out to make the world a better place for everyone.

Move Fast and Break Things

As with Jobs, such a mission starts to take on messianic overtones. Probably within Facebook, at its California HQ and spreading out across the world among its 50,000 or so employees, there is a respect and a fervour shown towards its founder and CEO. It is here, at the self-consciously nerdy and edgy address 1 Hacker Way, that Facebook seeks to continue its self-styled mission to 'Move Fast and Break Things'. That's easily done when it's a team of six, including the likes of (the future) Napster founder Sean Parker. But moving fast and breaking things when you are a $70 billion corporation, dominant in the majority of countries around the world? That is both risky and difficult.

And this is at the heart of why Facebook is such a combustible combination of ambition, self-styled maverick behaviour and a yearning for a higher purpose. All three of these elements can be seen in Zuckerberg's attitudes and actions. Without getting too psychoanalytical, it's clear that his ambition is driven, at least to some degree, by an ongoing need to continually prove that he isn't just another nerd in his bedroom.

Cambridge Analytica

The maverick behaviour, the desire to break things, has led to some rash decisions, some of which cross the boundaries of the law. The most notorious of these, from the last few years, is the Cambridge Analytica episode of 2018, which resulted in Facebook paying $5 billion in fines to the US federal authorities and £500,000 to UK data authorities.

As we have seen in previous stories, it is conspiracy and cover-up that are always more damning and damaging than the original crime. This is also the case with the Cambridge Analytica story. The whole episode started out as a small, controlled, transparent exercise. Cambridge Analytica invited Facebook users, using a process of informed consent, to take part in a survey via a neat little app, '*This is Your Digital Life*'. The survey was to be for academic purposes only, and participants would receive a small fee for taking part; 270,000 Facebook users responded and completed the survey. So far, so unremarkable.

It is what happened next that is certainly maverick, but also reveals the extent of Facebook's obsession with acquiring data. Facebook allowed this app to collect personal information from each respondent's database of Facebook Friends. In this way, the number of people whose data was harvested mushroomed from 270,000 to 87 million. Right there is a statistic showing the power (to Facebook) of 'bringing people together'.

The data that was acquired from these millions of users was sufficiently detailed enough to be able to build up a profile of susceptibility to certain types of advertising. Advertising to persuade us to buy certain products or services – we all more or less accept that this is the pact with the devil we have made with Facebook. You give us an amazing free platform and we'll help fund it by responding to paid ads.

The difficulty with Cambridge Analytica's application of the data was that it was sold to be used for political purposes, with the presidential nomination campaigns of Ted Cruz and Donald Trump in 2016 both making use of the granular detail available to them. The extent to which those campaigns materially benefited from the use of this data will never be known, but it was this that made legislators sit up and take notice.

It turned out that there are serious inconsistencies in the timeline of what was known, and when, about this whole messy affair within Facebook, leading to accusations of cover-up and obfuscation that go to the very top. After enquiries and various *mea culpa* statements from Facebook over several months, Zuckerberg finally testified before the House Energy and Commerce Committee in April 2018, at a hearing titled *Facebook: Transparency and Use of Consumer Data*. A 747-page transcript is available of the hearing, which, in the end, served up Zuckerberg with a load of pat-ball questions from committee members whose level of tech savviness offered, shall we say, something to be desired: questions included 'Why am I suddenly seeing chocolate ads all over Facebook? Do I have as many friends as I think I do?' Zuckerberg declined three times to appear at the UK's equivalent parliamentary committee of Culture, Media and Sport, an unprecedented snub that outraged the British government. Their lines of questioning are notoriously detailed and probing, which may have contributed to Zuckerberg's decision not to attend.

Facebook does what it does

In the end, the only conclusion that can be drawn from the Analytica episode is that it has merely confirmed what Facebook is good at: acquiring detailed personal data and then extracting and exploiting it. It was not a failure or a breach, it was what Facebook does, and continues to do. In March 2019, after the dust had settled and the 20 per cent dive in Facebook traffic following the Analytica PR disaster had been long recovered from, Zuckerberg delivered to the world his new 'privacy-focused' vision for Facebook and social networking. The *Guardian*'s Emily Bell pithily summarized the 3,000-word document as 'the nightmarish college application essay of an accomplished sociopath'.

Like any trained politician, Zuckerberg was contrite, spoke warmly, made some nice promises … and fundamentally did nothing. Facebook's biggest privacy-focused 'promise' has been to integrate its three messaging platforms – WhatsApp, Instagram and Messenger – into one, thereby incorporating the end-to-end encryption, which is such a strong feature of WhatsApp, into the other two. This neatly binds the three together, thus cannily making it far more difficult for the company to be broken up and have its dominance dismantled by offloading WhatsApp or Instagram, or both. At the end of December 2019, the US Federal Trade Commission considering asking a court to stop Facebook going ahead with this integration, but the company moved forward with the plan in 2020.

We're now left with the situation where Mark Zuckerberg's influence and philosophy dominate the chosen direction of Facebook as much as it ever did. Facebook's revenue growth is as eye-watering as ever: Q3 advertising revenue in 2020 rose to more than $21 billion. WhatsApp and Instagram dominate their sectors of the social media world as strongly as Facebook has a hold over its own, if not more so. Yet we are confronted with a similar ideological conflict at the heart of Facebook as we identified at Apple. There, a ruthless desire to entrap consumers in the Apple walled garden was disguised as an invitation to be part of the cool kids' gang. At Facebook, a ruthless desire to extract and monetize data (a Bezos desire, too, as we shall see) is disguised as some sort of utopian desire to 'give people voice and bring people together'.

So what?

OK, so what? In the run-up to the US presidential elections in November 2020, Facebook continued to fiercely defend the placing of political advertising on its platform. The last time around, in January 2016, Facebook's COO, Sheryl Sandberg, announced to investors that the 2016 election was 'a big deal in terms of ad spend'. She highlighted just what Cambridge Analytica was already at that time enabling: 'Using Facebook and Instagram ads you can target by congressional district, you can target by interest, you can target by demographics or any combination of those.'

The cynical targeting of voter groups; the Facebook platform as a home for fake news (as opposed to Trump's characterization of respected news outlets such as CNN and the *Washington Post* as 'fake news'); the dangerous echo chamber confirmation it provides for hate speech, misogyny and racism, no matter how hard the Facebook moderators work; and the downright intrusiveness and pervasiveness of the exploitation of our data – all this and more is Facebook's current legacy. Oh, and add to that Facebook's record of paying taxes. It shares form on this with Apple, Google, Amazon and others, but, as just one example, in its most recently reported financial year, in the UK Facebook paid just £28 million tax on revenues of £1.6 billion.

The hubristic warning sign that seems evident is a belief that the rules were not meant for them. Pause for a moment and reflect: all of the above situations have come about as a result of Mark Zuckerberg's decision-making. His conduct is that of someone who sees himself as above the law, too big and too important to be governed by any country's individual tax or regulatory authorities. He has learned to believe his own worldview, his own hype.

In the face of all this, millions of users would have cancelled their subscriptions years ago. Except there is no subscription to cancel, no direct debit to stop paying and so, on the basis of inertia and habit (and it's a habit that is hard to kick, as we stare down at our phones), we keep rewarding Facebook with even more data, even more Likes, even more content and advertising revenue.

King Zuck

All this keeps King Zuck in his castle, as proud, driven and ambitious as the hard-to-like college kid in *The Social Network*. Jobs' hubris, at its basic level, has merely hurt the wallets of several million overpaying Apple users, but has bestowed a speedier arrival of cooler, smarter tech from which we can all benefit, as competitors scrabbled to keep up with his dizzying vision.

Zuck's hubris, however, has inflicted far more wide-ranging damage on the world. The unprecedented invasion of our privacy (disguised as some sort of liberation); the promulgation and spread of fake news; the explosion of every form of cyber-bullying; an entire millennial generation's new obsession with appearance; and many other modern ills.

Like Apple, Facebook is a company that has been built on the very personal and dominant leadership of one individual. Zuckerberg's unwillingness to admit to the misjudgements and errors that have taken place over the past several years, is a reflection on what can happen when there are few safeguards, and few checks and balances to prevent a myth-creating engine from becoming reality.

It is yet another study in hypocrisy, dressing up a quest for world domination as nothing more than a desire to 'bring the world closer together'. As with Jobs' walled garden, at some point the scales will fall from all of our eyes. Either that, or they will fall from the eyes of regulators and Facebook will be broken up. In the meantime, the Facebook CEO has at least 30 more years to reach even greater heights, if only in his own head.

Case study 3: Jeff Bezos

As with Zuckerberg, Amazon's founder Jeff Bezos can also lay claim to touching the lives of millions around the world. Though 2021 sees him step aside as CEO, his continued success, plus his branching out into other interests such as the *Washington Post* and space exploration, show that his ambition and vision are limitless. Is his wealth, power and influence a force for good, or, in an increasingly values- and purpose-driven culture, are the seeds of Amazon's downfall already in evidence?

King of the world

It's hard not to get rather overwhelmed by the superlatives surrounding Bezos and Amazon. In early 2020 Amazon and the various parts of its empire held pole position in a number of key business measurements. Amazon is the world's largest online marketplace, cloud computing platform and AI assistant provider, as measured by market capitalization and by revenue. It is the largest Internet company in the world, again by revenue. It first achieved the magic trillion-dollar market capitalization milestone in September 2018, just a few months after Apple was the first company to hit that figure. It is roughly double the size of what can be regarded as its only serious global rival, China's Alibaba.

In a league table published in January 2020, Bezos was crowned, for the third year, as the richest man in the world, with a net worth in excess of $115 billion. This is even after Bezos' divorce in 2019 when he had to pay out $38 billion to ex-wife Mackenzie, making her, at a stroke, one of the richest women in the world.

So, when you are as rich as Croesus, what continues to drives you and what has actually driven you from the outset to that position? Unlike the seemingly more modest and generous Bill Gates, who Bezos has jostled with for this dizzying top spot, Bezos is somehow a more complex and conflicted character, one not immune to the dark allure of hubris.

It's all about data

So, Bezos and his love of data. Put simply, the reason Amazon is at least double the worth of Facebook is that Bezos has used the power of knowing everything about us to directly sell us more stuff, whereas Zuckerberg uses that same power to help other businesses to sell us more stuff. In that sense, Bezos has cut out the data middleman, just as he has cut out all the middlemen in every conceivable sector in which he operates. The 'middlemen' of wholesalers, retailers, bricks-and-mortar premises and dedicated product websites are all being swept away by the Amazon One Click solution.

Bezos doesn't sell data because he already owns it. The genius recognition that if I recommend a book to you that matches the taste of the one you have just bought, so that you're likely to buy two books instead of one, is really where the growth of Amazon started and, in many ways, is what it is still based on. It's just been scaled up to apply to every single product you are ever likely to want in your life. 'The Everything Store' indeed. Couple that with impeccable customer service (have you ever had a picking error from Amazon? Probably not), and it's not hard to understand why Amazon is now the juggernaut that it is.

Hollywood Jeff

Publicity photos of Bezos from the early days of Amazon show a pale, unathletic-looking guy, conservatively dressed in regulation chinos and button-down shirt, often surrounded by piles of books. But books were always just a means to an end, chosen as the first products to sell because they were hard to damage in the post and because online you could offer an exponential level of choice compared to the average bookstore.

Cut to tabloid pictures of Bezos in 2020, buffed up, wearing flamboyant jackets, glamorous new girlfriend Lauren Sanchez on his arm, photographed with Hollywood A-listers, celebrating his recent purchase of a mansion (built in the 1930s for Warner Brothers mogul Jack Warner) for a cool $165 million and we can see that his transformation is complete. And why not?

Why not indeed. Who wouldn't indulge themselves a little when they have that sort of cash in the bank? Let's not indulge in the politics of envy but instead just take a cool look at his journey and his track record in relation to treating people along the way with fairness and decency – surely as good a measurement as any against which to judge accusations of hubris.

The two-pizza rule

Back in 1998, four years after the launch of Amazon and the year it started branching out into selling music and videos as well as books, Bezos began publishing an annual letter for Amazon shareholders in which he started referring to five guiding principles for the business. These were:

1. focus on customers rather than on competitors
2. take risks in order to achieve market dominance
3. build staff morale
4. create a solid company culture
5. empower people

This last one came to be symbolized by one of the most vivid and simple business maxims ever to emerge from a corporate business: the two-pizza rule. This was the rule that every internal team should be small enough that it can be fed with two pizzas. If we're looking for an enduring legacy, wouldn't we all like to be the person who is known for coming up with that? In fact, all five principles are unarguably great ones to adhere to in creating a successful, dynamic, innovative, ethical and purpose-driven business in the twenty-first century and, more importantly, are based on the use of everyday language in contrast to the typically well-crafted statements many of us are more used to seeing.

Scaling up

In whatever clever way the internal workings of Amazon were structured, this has seemed to ensure that its three most significant points of expansion have been cannily organic, creating the maximum efficiency in implementing them.

1. How to expand into just about every market sector there is without scaling up the buying team? Create Marketplace and let third-party sellers take the strain for you.

2. You have invested heavily in data processing and server infrastructure, but how could this work even harder for you? Create a business that sells this to third parties. Hence Amazon Web Services (AWS) was born.

3. With a business that processes an order book so large and complex, there is a need to go beyond standard computer power and employ AI to anticipate and solve certain issues. So, through a blend of know-how acquisitions and a focus of resources, create an AI division which will spawn Echo and Alexa.

So, instead of reinventing the wheel or getting diverted down alluring cul-de-sacs, Amazon just keeps adding more wheels which make the juggernaut go faster down the same basic road to profit, driving all other traffic off the road.

No level playing field

It is that road-hog mentality that brings us to the dark side of Amazon. While it is not unusual for tech companies to acquire a crazy market capitalization even in the face of massive and persistent balance sheet losses, it is unusual for one that is, fundamentally, just another retailer. Its ultra-aggressive stance towards its margins, persistently underselling competitors and happy to live with zero profit in every sector until it has achieved market-share dominance, is unprecedented. Couple that with another aspect it shares with tech stock companies – an at best 'creative' and at worst 'evasive' attitude towards paying tax in local jurisdictions – and two of the price governors for most retail businesses are suddenly avoided. Add to that no need to pay rent on property or business rates, or employ shop staff, and it's not hard to understand why Amazon is almost single-handedly hollowing out every high street and driving small independent retailers to the wall.

Prime time

To capitalize on all of this still further, Bezos, in a trick from the Jobs playbook, has created his own walled garden, Amazon Prime. In the world of Prime, everything becomes even easier, even more frictionless, even more habitual so that it is now second nature to buy things and be entertained too via streamed services. Millions of us pay good money every month to be allowed into the Amazon Prime amusement park, not even noticing that it has gates and is enclosed by a wall. And so Amazon's relentlessness continues, penetrating deeper into every available market around the world, selling every conceivable product and service.

The balance sheet

So, right now, what is the reckoning? What is the judgement now and what will it be in the future on Amazon, Bezos and its legacy?

There is, of course, a long and complicated balance sheet to evaluate in relation to Bezos and Amazon and its relentless progress, which is well documented in articles and think pieces online.

'A sickly gazelle'

Back in the early 2000s, when selling books still represented a significant portion of its sales, Amazon achieved market dominance in ways that can only be described as ruthless. In his book *The Everything Store*, Brad Stone outlines how small publishers leapt at the chance to gain access to this incredible new distribution channel and signed up with Amazon. However, in what would become a familiar story, once these publishers became dependent on Amazon for their sales, Amazon, Stone claims, would demand extended payment terms and bigger discounts. Publishers who didn't sign up to such terms would find their books suddenly harder to find on the site and listed at higher prices, thus depressing sales.

Amazon's relationship with these small, vulnerable publishers was referred to internally as The Gazelle Project, following Bezos apparently stating that Amazon 'should approach these small publishers the way a cheetah would pursue a sickly gazelle'. Amazon's legal team balked at such a grizzly metaphor and demanded that the project be given a more anodyne name, the Small Publishers Negotiation Program.

Looking at what has happened since, you feel that Bezos is capable of having regarded the global supply of products and services as full of sickly gazelles meekly waiting to be hunted down by his fleet-footed big cat.

Bezos Earth Fund

On the flip side of the balance sheet, suddenly announced in February 2020 with little additional fanfare was the Bezos Earth Fund, launched with an initial donation of $10 billion.

Bezos announced, 'Climate change is the biggest threat to our planet', and 'I want to work alongside others both to amplify known ways and to explore new ways of fighting the devastating impact of climate change on this planet we all share.'

Here, finally, is a man in his 50s who has a dawning realization that ultimately, for someone in his position, it is all about legacy. Bezos is savvy enough to accept that Amazon's success may end up being relatively fleeting. 'If you look at large companies, their lifespans tend to be 30-plus years, not a hundred-plus years,' he said in 2018, recognizing the faster rise and fall cycle of businesses in the past few decades. He has also said that he would be grateful if its success lasted at least until he died. It is worth noting that the average life span of an S&P company today is about 12–15 years.

On that basis, Bezos is smart enough to realize that his true legacy may not be the Amazon business, but what goes on beyond it. Bill Gates has recognized that, too, with the currently far more ambitious (in scope and scale) Bill & Melinda Gates Foundation. And Bezos, like Musk, has decided that space exploration is a cool bit of legacy-building to get into via his Blue Origin project.

Too little, too late?

To his sternest critics, initiatives such as the Bezos Earth Fund and Amazon's 2018 decision to raise its minimum wage to closer to a living wage, are just window dressing. However, even Bernie Sanders, one of Amazon's harshest political critics in the US, was moved to applaud Amazon for being one of the first major employers to accede to the demands of the 'Fight for $15' fair wage campaign.

There are, then, some signs of mellowing, of softening, of casting an eye on the judgement history will make on Amazon and on Jeff Bezos. But along the way the price, for many, has been heavy and the charge sheet is long. Booksellers decimated, with many, possibly most, retail sectors not far behind in their decline in the wake of Amazon. Persistent accusations of tough working conditions for Amazon warehouse staff and delivery drivers. A continuing compliance with just the letter and not the spirit of the law in terms of paying tax dues in local jurisdictions. An aggressive harvesting of personal data with which many feel uncomfortable. A failure to block hateful content published on Kindle or in third party reseller products. And a blind eye turned to fake reviews.

Failure and curiosity

Amazon has, perhaps better than some other companies, been quick both to accept failures and be constantly curious. Let's consider Bezos' willingness to accept and embrace failure. For example, take Amazon Fire phone – a significant investment that was quickly dissolved upon the realization that it would not deliver its intended promise. The decision to shut it down was the very opposite of hubristic behaviour. Rather than become locked into pursuing a business innovation, purely out of pride or ego, or an unwillingness to accept that the idea was not going to work, Bezos shut it down, acknowledging that failure is part of the DNA, and modelling a humility that basically accepted that you won't always get it right.

The acquisition of Zappos is perhaps the best example of the learning curve that Bezos has created at Amazon. While many feared that Zappos would morph into an Amazonian stepchild, Bezos was quick to point out that the acquisition was not about world domination but about learning from a company that was better than they were in the areas of customer obsession and logistics management. This curiosity, a desire to seek to learn, rather than believe that Amazon already had all the answers, provides a counterbalance to the challenges of hubris that can be laid at Bezos' door.

Jeff Bezos is in charge

Jeff Bezos isn't some aloof figurehead, coasting along on the back of some greatest hits 20 years ago. He was in total hands-on control throughout his time as CEO of Amazon and so anything that occurred on his watch had his fingerprints on it.

His belated forays into philanthropy and good causes are behind that of a figure like Bill Gates, but probably not that far different from fellow self-obsessed nerds like Mark Zuckerberg. Blue Origin –

a private spaceflight company founded in 2000 by Bezos – is, so far, more vanity project than contributor to the sum of human happiness. Bezos' acquisition of the *Washington Post*, while it has been successful within its limited terms, seems a mild diversion into being a media mogul rather than a full-blown tilt at becoming the next Murdoch.

To all intents and purposes, his central drive remains the continuation and expansion of Amazon's worldwide dominance.

What can stop Amazon?

His laser-like focus, after 25 years, on the continuing and relentless expansion of Amazon is ultimately a little awe-inspiring and possibly even scary, and not just for his rivals. This is entrepreneurship taken to a level that we have never seen before. It is ambition on stilts to which enforcers of US anti-trust laws have so far been remarkably supine in reacting. There continue to be predictions that Amazon will be forced to be 'broken up' in a bid to curb its power. And yet Amazon sailed through the billion-dollar valuation and beyond with no discernible reaction from Capitol Hill. Former President Trump, goaded by jibes from the *Washington Post*, saw Amazon and Bezos as a liberal-elite threat, but seemed to realize he had no real powers to limit Amazon's expansion.

So what will stop Amazon? At the time of writing, we are currently experiencing the seismic effects of a global pandemic, which has led to the shutdown of major economies around the world. For some businesses and sectors, this spells catastrophe. Of the subjects so far featured in this book, many are suffering some painful consequences. For some or all of Boeing, WeWork, General Motors, Uber, Deutsche Bank and Apple, these shutdowns may even prove damaging in the long run. But guess whose business is booming? Yup, with that uncanny and unerring ability to be in the right place at the right time, buying online, probably through Amazon, is one of the primary shopping avenues that remains open, with customers flocking there more than ever before.

Jeff Bezos' hubris

So where does all this place Bezos in relation to hubristic behaviour and its effect on Amazon and wider society? Looking at his accumulated wealth and Amazon's assets, Bezos and Amazon could afford to fix everything that is wrong in its business. Its working conditions, its treatment of suppliers and even competitors, its policing of the content on its platforms, its care over the use of its customers' data – all these things and more, with the right focus and resources, could be cleaned up and placed on a less aggressive and ruthlessly acquisitive footing. And at a moment in our history when all our taxes are sorely needed to invest in healthcare and providing a financial safety net for vast swathes of the population, how about paying more tax, too.

All this would cost Amazon money, margin and profit to fix but probably not enough to wound it or appreciably slow it down. And maybe, just maybe, the empire might attract back some of that (admittedly small) band of Amazon boycotters.

On that basis, the charge that sticks is one that a continuing cheetah-pursuing-gazelle view of the world is promulgated, endorsed and promoted by Bezos himself. And in this it is a display of overbearing ambition, of pride and, yes, of hubris. Amazon can be seen as the ultimate expression of Western capitalism's Darwinian 'survival of the fittest'. Darwin understood that this maxim also had to fit within a complex ecosystem, populated by a vast array of interdependent biodiversity. However, just as human activity is degrading the diversity of species around the world at an alarming rate, so Amazon is degrading the commercial choice and diversity available to us. Its namesake, the Amazon river and rainforest, is perhaps the ultimate symbol of the world's fragility and interdependence and therefore a choice of company name that is in danger of seeming highly ironic.

Amazon's agreement to the 'Fight for $15' campaign is a chink of light, a sign that perhaps a more rounded, less aggressive and less ambitious Amazon may emerge in the 2020s. When someone is on the top of the podium year after year, endlessly winning starts to lose its allure and some generosity towards fellow competitors, for the good of the whole sport, can start to become more important. This is where Amazon and Bezos are right now. They have the chance, perhaps even the responsibility, to consider widening their outlook to take into consideration the social as well as the economic impact of their strategy and its implementation.

Whether Amazon and Bezos will continue the tentative steps down the path of understanding and accepting the full weight of corporate social responsibility that an organization of its size, power and reach should shoulder, remains to be seen. For the vast majority of its corporate existence, Amazon has been head-down, hellbent on expansion at any cost. The boundless, ruthless ambition of its founder, with his cool calculation that data is the ultimate source of power in the Internet age, is, looking at his peers, still unrivalled.

However, sentiment towards a brand, its aura and its halo, can shift surprisingly fast, as Bezos acknowledged in his 'lifecycle' timescale view of current businesses. That, along with the possibility that the anti-trust bear in the US might just be poked once too often and roar into action, means that Amazon's future success is by no means guaranteed.

It could just be that all the goodwill towards Amazon, which has been bought from customers at cheap prices rather than earned through respect, is merely skin deep. Its owner's values may be ones of honesty, decency and fairness but to the average outsider such attributes may well not be what come to mind when asked to sum up Amazon.

Case study 4: Elon Musk

A controversial figure from the outset of his career, Elon Musk may be in the process of making the transition from maverick outsider to that of a pillar of the automotive industry. Musk's ambitions seem limitless, including his shared ambition with Bezos to venture into space exploration. Has Musk successfully walked the hubris tightrope?

Musk strikes us as being a combination of a fan and a practitioner. This makes him prone to excessive displays of both tendencies, but, in an odd way, this also personifies perhaps greater transparency, more of a 'what you see is what you get' scenario, which you could argue makes him seem a more rounded individual than the subjects of our three other case studies. Musk and Tesla remain very much on an upward trajectory, rather than in the relatively mature phase being experienced by Apple, Facebook and Amazon. No longer a start-up, of course, but at a point where there is still a chance of crash and burn just as much as there is of sector dominance. This makes an assessment of Elon Musk, his personality and his position on the hubris scale particularly interesting; he is still at a point where things could go either way.

Wayward and unpredictable

And that is emblematic of the man, someone who is wayward, unpredictable, inconsistent, often downright hypocritical. He is inspiring and infuriating, often within the same interview or press conference. He does not shy away from the trappings of fame and fortune: his colourful showbiz-linked private life and cameo appearances in favourite TV shows are just some of the indicators that he relishes having become a brand and a personality. At first glance, many of the traits – wayward, unpredictable, inconsistent, and hypocritical – are often those that indicate hubris, so why might that be different for Musk? As with the other case studies, we need to look at his track record in order to answer the question we are asking ourselves.

Tesla's fast-lane progress

Does any of this matter? Will Elon Musk have a lasting influence on the commercial life of the US and beyond in the 2020s and decades beyond that? We wouldn't bet against it. Let's consider the light-speed transformation in the fortunes of the two auto manufacturers most familiar to the man in the street: Ford and Tesla. The company Henry

Ford founded in 1903, and in the Model T employed assembly line production for the first time, had a market capitalization in mid-2018 of just over $50 billion. Tesla, the company Elon Musk has helmed since 2008 then had a similar market cap, but overtook Ford in 2018. That milestone moment, the upstart edging past the establishment, was considered remarkable at the time.

Look at what has happened since that bisecting of the valuations, with Tesla leaving Ford as a diminishing speck in its rear-view mirror as it speeds off (silently, electrically) into the distance. Even in the midst of the market turbulence caused by the coronavirus (or perhaps even because of it) Tesla's market cap was at a staggering $130 billion in April 2020 while Ford's had shrunk to just $21 billion. Tesla is therefore worth more than *six times* that of Ford in the eyes of investors. With General Motors also having shrunk to a $33 billion market cap, Tesla is edging towards being worth three times the combined worth of the US's two fallen automotive giants. As a further indication of the magnitude of its reach and success, Tesla is now worth nearly double that of Volkswagen and is second only to Toyota in the world automakers' league table.

The move to electric

Even by the standards of an Apple or an Amazon, the meteoric rise, shown in the numbers and an amazing ascent at rocket speed (an apt metaphor for Musk), makes it difficult now not to pause and stare in awe. Driven no doubt by a shrewd understanding of regulations and with all the market-force stars aligned in its favour, Tesla is now reaping the benefits of governments around the world setting tough targets for the replacement of internal combustion engine cars and light vehicles with electric ones. The UK government has pushed its already aggressive target date for this switch from 2040 down to 2035, a mere 15 years away at the time of writing, and a number of countries are even pressing for 2030 as the cut-off date for the sales of petrol and diesel cars. The US, under climate crisis denier

President Trump, failed to produce any federal legislation up to 2020, but President Joe Biden has returned the US to the Paris climate accord and individual cities and states are coming up with their own initiatives. Los Angeles has legislated for all buses to be electric by 2025 and all new vehicles by 2030. This is a seismic shift that Tesla saw coming and, it can be argued, has even influenced the scale and speed of its implementation.

To understand hubris in this context, we would argue that it is in fact the rest of the automotive industry that has displayed hubris. A blindness and an arrogance that made the traditional manufacturers believe that the sanctity of the petrol car – its central place in American life, its symbolism as a provider of freedom, choice and the open road – would surely mean that it still had a long and healthy life.

To accelerate the move to electric, the tax regimes of various countries are offering incredible incentives, which even Tesla at its most optimistic could not have anticipated. The UK is considering major changes to company car tax in favour of electric vehicles. As of 6 April 2020, company car users in the UK who choose an all-electric vehicle pay no company car tax at all. With over 50 per cent of car sales in the UK going to fleet buyers, this is an amazing incentive. Over the past couple of decades, the perk of a company car has been steadily eroded by a ramping up of company car tax. At a stroke, this provides Tesla with a massive sales benefit: on a Tesla Model S versus a similarly priced Mercedes-Benz petrol car, a user will save several thousand pounds a year in tax! Of course, a tax structure change like this is designed to incentivize all manufacturers to go electric, but Tesla, with its existing model choices, production capacity and superior mileage range on one charge, is already significantly ahead of the game.

Just as they missed the warning signs of Asian manufacturers ever being likely to undermine their hegemony in the US, now, second time around, it seems that many automotive companies may have missed the boat regarding the electric revolution. But at least some of the sleeping giants have now stirred to go all out to play catch-up on battery technology and design. However, just as Jobs, Zuckerberg and Bezos before him have understood the massive benefit of early sector dominance, so Musk is now reaping those same rewards.

The car iPhone

If Zuckerberg and Bezos are selling a service, it is Jobs and Musk who are manufacturers of products, and very cool ones at that. There is a similar 'cool premium' added to (and achieved by) Tesla cars as there is to iPhones, and that has clearly been a deliberate policy from the outset – go niche, cool and premium to start with, then go mass-market with lower-cost models, but only when the more mass-market models benefit from the premium models' aura of luxury and exclusiveness. It's a classic marketing tactic but one that Tesla has pulled off well. There have been wobbles along the way, with delays in ramping up production and some technical issues dogging Tesla's progress. However, the market clearly thinks that these problems are largely behind them, and their increased production capacity is continuing at an impressive pace.

The rise of the gigafactory

Tesla cars aren't produced in mere factories, but in self-styled gigafactories, vast assembly complexes that are astonishing in their scale and design. So much so that Gigafactory 1, in Sparks, Nevada, has expanded to become, at 15 million square feet, the largest building in the world. With gigafactories built or planned in New York, Shanghai and Berlin, Tesla's plans for automotive world domination are clear … and, more importantly, are being delivered.

All of the above points to leadership innovation, and an ability to seek new and different ways to lead an organization to success.

Musk hubris?

So is the man at the head of all this a hubristic megalomaniac or a visionary environmentalist, working to save the planet no less?

As with Jobs, Zuckerberg and Bezos, the answer isn't exactly clear-cut. Musk is a bewildering 'pick and mix' of contradictions, a wily operator who hedges his bets and adopts a chameleon-like persona to further his ends. He is a major donor to both the Republican and the Democratic parties in the US. He sees himself as an environmentalist whose emissions-free vehicles will make a real difference to the fight against global warming. And yet he is openly disdainful of public transport, the expansion of which is surely a bigger influence on transport's carbon footprint. He has made political donations to Republicans who are openly anti-environmental. He has stated that he is against state subsidies while benefiting massively from them in the setting up of some of his gigafactories and in some of his SpaceX activities.

He has displayed a similarly Janus-like attitude to artificial intelligence. On the one hand he has referred to AI as 'the most serious threat to the survival of the human race'. On the other in 2015 he set up OpenAI, a not-for-profit AI research company, and in 2016 he co-founded Neuralink, a neurotechnology company whose aim is to integrate the human brain with artificial intelligence. As such, it would seem that, to Musk, the world cannot be trusted to develop AI safely unless it is under the auspices of a superior intelligence, i.e. Musk himself. Here, surely, is something of a display of arrogance, a hubristic belief that only he can control the AI genie now that it is out of the bottle.

Musk has an impressive track record as an innovative and shrewd philanthropist, supporting forward-looking and impactful causes which can make a real difference. Brought right up to date, he has been a leading responder to the coronavirus crisis, repurposing his space programme team at SpaceX to manufacture and distribute face masks and protective suits. Tesla also turned over some of its manufacture to producing ventilators for use in hospitals.

The flip side even here, though, resulted in probably the most notorious episode of Musk's career to date. The dramatic rescue of a junior football team trapped in a cave in Thailand in 2018 made headlines around the world. Musk put to use the underwater expertise of his engineers at The Boring Company and SpaceX to design, build and ship a mini-submarine to assist in the rescue. Although never used, his efforts were recognized and rewarded by the King of Thailand. So far, so admirable and philanthropic. However, the mini-sub was criticized by one of the rescue team advisers as being no more than a publicity stunt. Musk, who has a hair-trigger response on Twitter to many issues, made negative references about the advisor, resulting in a massive backlash, court cases and defamation settlements.

Vain or enlightened?

Is this a display of thin-skinned vanity, something that seems to cloud the judgement of so many influential individuals these days? Trump, Zuckerberg, Jobs, Bezos, Neumann at WeWork, Wagoner at GM ... all have displayed vainglorious behaviour of one sort or another. This is the flashpoint where the cult of personality meets the frailty of human nature. Propagating your own cult of personality, as all these figures have done or continue to do, leads to a combustible situation where an air of infallibility creeps in, a dangerous harbinger of hubris. Musk now finds himself in the position of being at the forefront of the future of the entire world's automotive industry, surely as powerful a place to be, in its own way, as that of Zuckerberg and Bezos. Will he use this as a force for good? He is too much a self-styled maverick figure for this to be an easy question to answer.

On balance, we would be willing to give Musk the benefit of the doubt at the moment. Unlike an unimaginative moneyman like Wagoner at GM, Musk is at least aiming, SpaceX-style, for the stars. He has vision, passion and enthusiasm, infectious qualities that inspire loyalty and admiration within Tesla and a growing cohort of loyal Tesla customers. His SpaceX project, of any of the non-NASA space initiatives, looks potentially the most imaginative and technologically brilliant. Footage of his Tesla Roadster with a dummy astronaut in orbit has to be one of the most inspiring pieces of space footage since Chris Hadfield sang 'Space Oddity' in the International Space Station. And footage of the successful landing of one of the SpaceX reusable rockets on a tiny drone ship in the ocean is just a jaw-dropping piece of precision tech ballet.

The cult of personality

Just as a political system which depends disproportionately on the personality of its leader can be seen to have its vulnerabilities (a massive understatement, clearly), then our model of modern commerce is similarly precarious.

Looking back at all four of these case studies, this is where we find ourselves in the 2020s – the business mogul as showbiz personality. And just as entertainment stars have an above average chance of succumbing to the weaknesses of vanity and the temptations thrown up by too much money and a fawning entourage, so too can the modern business leader crash and burn.

While the household names we've discussed earlier in this chapter are at the narrow apex of this business hierarchy, there is an inherent risk that millions of business leaders and entrepreneurs out there are beguiled by the example they set and start to see themselves as the next Musk or Bezos and seek to emulate their approaches. There have always been larger-than-life moguls, as exemplified by William Randolph Hearst's portrayal, in the character of Charles Foster Kane, in Orson Welles Citizen Kane. But the reach and influence of Hearst/Kane is small fry compared with our quartet here; our four have all affected our lives to varying degrees.

In later chapters, we'll talk more about the checks and balances needed to be put in place to ensure that any budding Bezoses, Musks and others are channelled correctly. We need to find ways to ensure that their originality, energy and ingenuity are not stifled while at the same time developing an environment for them to operate in; one of co-operation, reflection and collaboration that serves an organization effectively and doesn't just feed an individual ego. If handled correctly, this combination can be unbeatable and a sustainable model for the long term. If this tricky balancing act is not achieved, then the ego and hubris of an all-powerful leader can bring down the entire organization.

While examples of hubris in entrepreneurial CEOs can be found in many organizations, it is illuminating for the reader to benchmark examples they may know against the performance of four of the most well-known entrepreneurs of the past 30 years.

CHAPTER 5

The Damage Hubris Inflicts

Too much power in CEOs' hands

While Jobs, Zuckerberg, Bezos and Musk have had the magic touch (at least some of the time), millions of other executives now yearn to acquire similar megastar status. In the process, they may start to believe their own hype and seek to limit the power of others within an organization. Looking at the examples of businesses such as Amazon and Tesla, it is easy to start believing that the best model for success is one in which a charismatic, visionary, determined CEO can lead an organization to success by having a singular, distinctive strategy.

However, because of the extensive media coverage generated by the likes of Bezos and Musk, the role of the visionary genius may be perceived as being more common than it is. Let's try to put things into perspective. A handful of these guys come along once in a generation, not by the battalion-load out of MIT and Harvard. Just as it is easy to forget how exceptional Federer, Nadal and Djokovic are in tennis, because they all happen to be playing in the same decades, if you're an organization holding out for a clear-eyed saviour who will cut through your sector and lift you to the top, you probably have a long wait ahead of you.

These guys are as rare as hen's teeth. If you're in the automobile business or in retail, there's more likelihood of a Musk or a Bezos simply swallowing you up in one of their casual acquisitions than your new CEO version of them arriving in time to prevent that happening.

And then, even if some Bezos 2.0 were to mysteriously emerge and take charge, the trade-off of brilliance and originality needs to be incredibly high when set against the probable hubristic threat to the balance of power within your organization.

The golden hello

While such visionaries may be rare, there is still a strong desire and intent to find that spark of brilliance that can bring about something unique. Not surprisingly, many boards responsible for appointing CEOs will play their part in seeking out such talent. There is strong evidence throughout the corporate world that corporate governance continues to be a topic of debate. As recently as February 2021, boards were warned against being seduced into giving large pay increases to CEOs in the light of government bail-outs and reduced performance. Time will tell if the right checks and balances prevail. Meanwhile the new CEO's CV is as selectively read as it was selectively put together – highlighting past triumphs, however fleeting, and glossing over periods of failure, stasis and pursuing strategies up blind alleys. In the hunger for a saviour to guide the business through the market conditions we are all living through, i.e. where success is measured by the most recent set of results and whether you're right at the top of your sector, the gleam of the golden hello can be blinding to all parties.

The incoming CEO is showered with tempting rewards of bonuses and stock options and a salary package commensurate with what they bring to the table. Not dissimilar to the world of sport, highly-sought-after executives are courted and large 'transfer fees' (by buying out share packages) are easily accommodated to attract the best and the brightest. This is the corporate world behaving like the English Premier League transfer market, with a similar fixation on short-term results. No goals scored in your first three matches? Time for the subs bench already?

Winning the league

So, our expensive new signing has donned the number 9 shirt and is out on the pitch and inspiring some quick wins. Already the fans' (shareholders') favourite, the player then starts to believe his/her own hype even more than the board and the shareholders do. It is then, all too often, that the narrative arc of the new-signing, goal-scoring footballer and the incoming CEO starts to diverge.

In football, success breeds success, as the two key ingredients needed to sustain it are confidence and momentum. In the business world, things may be slightly different.

CEO honeymoon period

Well-run businesses find ways to nurture and develop momentum brought about by some level of success. If the confidence it creates can be spread sufficiently across the whole organization, you create a business where thousands of employees tap into the buzz and the energy of success, and the transformational power that can be unleashed will be phenomenal.

However, where the success is ascribed to and claimed by a single person, the CEO, it can have a distorting and ultimately damaging effect. If it is an early success, it all too often becomes the excuse to sit back and rest on laurels rather than having the humility to see it as probably one of three things:

1. First, it could be nothing more than luck: things falling into place just at the right time that are probably the result of groundwork undertaken by the CEO's predecessor.

2. Second, it could have come about as a result of the benefit of bringing a new and fresh perspective to the business, exactly what the CEO was brought in to achieve. However, that outsider perspective is always going to be a transitory, short-term benefit. The outsider all too quickly becomes an insider to that sector, as it is now the world in which the CEO is immersed and living, 24/7.

3. And finally, it is just a few successes, not a series of sustainable successes, achieved during a honeymoon period, which may be the first six months, perhaps the first couple of years, depending on the business's expectations in its results cycle. In that period there is a greater degree of freedom to operate, a greater willingness to allow the CEO to show their flair, resulting in less scrutiny, and finally more hunger by the board and by shareholders to play up any success, however minor.

The humble CEO should be quick to highlight which of these categories of winning any initial success falls into. The temptation for the hubristic CEO is to overclaim for success, again in any of the three categories into which it falls. The first one is to take all the glory even when it is really a team effort or an inherited benefit from the outgoing regime. This is the equivalent, in footballing terms, of hanging around in the penalty area for that half-chance rather than contributing to the build-up of the match.

The second one, revelling in the unique outsider's perspective, may well be a genuine success, but this so easily tips over into excessive pride that 'only I was able to see the wood for the trees'. Congratulations: in this quarter you have thoroughly earned the dazzling package you were brought in on. The problem is that this can quickly be reframed as you being superior to the rest; that the board, and other leaders before you, are mere pedestrians who lack the imagination and the wider experience to see what *really* needs to happen around here.

The third is the most common, however: trading on an early success and then, instead of using it as momentum to build on and develop, doing the exact opposite and sitting back and using it as a buffer from further pressure and scrutiny. It becomes a way to extend the honeymoon period way beyond what is healthy for the business. It may even be a disguised one-trick-pony approach, in that it could be a repeat of the key idea/technique that has worked at every business preceding this one on the CV. In other words, instead of demonstrating energy, originality and a hunger to improve and develop the business, it is the opposite of all these things. It is lazy, unoriginal and a safe fallback, but because it is new to this company or sector, it seems clever and the promise of more great things from this new CEO.

The insider or the outsider?

The combination of an incoming reward structure skewed towards short-term success, and a board craving a quick win, can easily play into the hands of the careerist CEO. This new post is just another bauble on the CV, a further rounding of the impressive track record of experience rather than a heartfelt desire to help and develop this business right now, in this sector.

This is always a major dilemma for CEO-appointment boards. Go for the seasoned industry insider, who can hit the ground running because they already work in the business or the sector? Or be willing to take a leap in the dark, bring in an outsider who will introduce that crucial extra level of perspective, the ability to take a sideways look at everything and question why things have always been done in a particular way.

The insider is far less likely to display hubristic tendencies, but is more likely to be a continuity candidate, bringing a safe progression on the existing strategy rather than a radical reappraisal and dramatic shake-up, maybe just when that is exactly what is needed.

The outsider comes with the whiff of the maverick, the radical thinker, the catalyst for long-overdue change: here's a new sheriff riding into town and the townsfolk are apprehensive but excited. And because those heady expectations are in place, the new CEO is keen to meet them, bringing in some changes surprisingly early, and making a mark.

The outsider makes their mark

This is where things can go either way. The change, the shake-up by the outsider, may be just what was needed, implemented in the nick of time. Divesting a division that was felt to be essential but was ultimately a drag on profitability and a distraction; accelerating the move online of key parts of the business; spotting growth markets that were not being targeted; making smarter use of customer data to add incremental sales (straight from the Bezos playbook); entering markets in new countries using intimate knowledge of their foibles; or flattening the organization's structure. All these are examples of typical outsider moves which may not have been properly identified by the existing board.

However, for each one of these examples, the law of unintended consequences can come along and bite back. Most large organizations have grown into businesses that are as complicated and intricate as a Swiss watch. Each part of the mechanism is finely tuned and balanced to work in conjunction with many other moving parts. Remove one seemingly innocuous cog, spring or spindle and suddenly the whole mechanism has stopped keeping time as accurately as it once did or may even stop working altogether.

Dismantling or restructuring is usually a one-way process; once it's done, it's done. You cannot simply put the spring back because you can no longer reach that part of the mechanism. Make an entire team redundant and that expertise is instantly dissipated, lost forever to competitors or other sectors. So, the 'making a mark' cost-cutting, efficiency-generating, structure-flattening move by the new CEO who brooks no counsel from others becomes a short-term win for the bottom line, but a medium- and long-term disaster in terms of lost expertise and know-how that has now flowed to your direct competitors.

Doubling down

The term 'doubling down' is one which is used more than ever these days, a perceived sign of strength and decisiveness and, in the face of logic, reason and often proven facts; a tactic for riding out any criticism by appearing to be even more convinced of your original position rather than bowing to any correction and suggestions of changing course. It is a favourite approach of former US president Donald Trump; look even stronger and more decisive by brushing aside all criticism, and resort to claims of 'fake news' as the reaction to any uncomfortable truths.

If it is good enough for the president of the United States, it's legitimate for the average corporate CEO or VP. The news cycle, in the business press as much as in any other part of the media, is on such a relentlessly fast turnaround that what makes headlines today as a gaffe or a misjudgement has blown over by the next day. Forceful denial, reiteration of a strongly stated position, even if plain wrong, often hidden behind a 'spokesperson for the organization', have become common tactics.

'Never complain, never explain'

The forceful and, let's face it, hubristic CEO resorts to doubling down as a way to ride out the news cycle until it moves on to someone or something else. Bluff, a hiding behind 'we abide by the guidelines' as a way of glossing over a tax, employment or health and safety failing: this is something we see everywhere. In a supposedly more reflective, aware and responsible world, doubling down and steamrollering through a controversy, in political and in commercial life, seems to be the tactic that is being deployed. On that basis, the rise of the shameless CEO is one that can be seen to be succeeding.

Like so many memorable quotes, 'Never complain, never explain' has been attributed to both Benjamin Disraeli and Winston Churchill but may well be far older than that. Whatever its source, it is certainly one that some leaders most likely have at their bedside, too. That is not to say that its opposite would be a recommended approach for a CEO either. That sounds like a recipe for never getting anything done, losing respect and getting bogged down in taking on board every axe-grinding opinion the CEO comes up against.

However, 'explain' should be part of the process of engaging the hearts and minds of the board, employees and other stakeholders. Sweeping in with new, radical ideas, if they can be explained and rationalized, will help gain acceptance and engender trust in the judgement of a new CEO. This is not weakness, it is strength – it is a different, healthier way to double down. It is backing up decisions with a secondary process of showing your workings, laying bare the reasons for your decision.

The virtue of transparency

Transparency has never been more valued by society than it is right now as politicians around the world are being challenged on the transparency of their approach to handling the coronavirus pandemic and are being seen to respond in sharply different ways.

In business, in an information age when everything is accessible via a quick and easy Google search, there is an increasing conflict emerging for CEOs and boards, just as there is for politicians. Leaks, rumours and premature disclosure can damage investor confidence and create unnecessary and distracting share price turbulence and investor speculation. It can also alert competitors to initiatives way before they are able to be used to good advantage by the originating company.

In such a potentially febrile atmosphere, it can be alarmingly easy for a CEO and the board to go into defensive mode, shutting down disclosure to a bare minimum, need-to-know basis, for employees and investors alike. It is interesting to note that as recently as November 2019, Labrador, a communications agency specializing in regulated disclosure documents, launched a US-based Transparency Awards, ranking all S&P 250 companies. The fact that there is even a need for awards such as this is an indication that transparency is seen as a virtue rather than the norm.

We have already shown that a lack of transparency is a hallmark of the style of management of many of the most hubristic episodes we have highlighted in this book so far. At the Labrador Transparency Awards a judgement is made against '4 pillars of transparency': the accessibility, accuracy, comparability and availability of information. The overall winner in 2019 was the Coca-Cola Company, a business recently criticized for its opaqueness in response to pressure to improve recycling initiatives in relation to the billions of single-use plastic bottles it produces each year. So maybe these awards focus on the letter of the law of transparency rather than the spirit. However, it is good to see General Motors as a category winner, yet another indication perhaps that Mary Barra and her team really have turned over a new leaf and are developing a more open, responsive, humble culture.

In Part 2 of this book, we will explore in more detail the value of transparency in increasing accountability and building trust among investors, employees and suppliers. It is one of the key defences against hubris. Explaining why something didn't work; admitting mistakes; sharing strategy and updating on progress, risk and opportunities – all these are the hallmarks of a more self-aware and rounded approach.

Protecting data or shielding reputations?

We have seen the power and value of data in the hands of shrewd data practitioners such as Zuckerberg and Musk. In an era of GDPR paranoia and the clamour for a right to be forgotten to really mean something, the leaking of data can be a weapon. The careful guarding and prudent use of data is an essential part of a business's reputation. But when is that line crossed, and 'privacy' just a more virtuous sounding way of expressing 'secrecy'?

Apple, Google, Facebook and Amazon probably handle cumulatively more personal data than any other companies in the world. And yet they each have a reputation for being opaque in their tax arrangements in local jurisdictions and in, for example, the clarity of their policies of handling whistleblowers. They manage to conflate data and privacy caution with a guardedness towards declaring policies on issues that should be more widely aired.

When you consider the concern that is often expressed around the intentions of China and Sovereign Wealth funds, it seems at odds with the level of scrutiny applied to the likes of Facebook. Paranoia surrounding the granting of 5G licences to Huawei and the reputation of Bank of China as one of the world's most secretive banks are just two examples of Western fear of China, driven almost entirely by a lack of transparency. As the success of Chinese companies around the world continues, as does that of the big tech companies, it may be tempting for a proud, domineering CEO to look at their examples and conclude that the PR downside of a lack of transparency is outweighed by what appears to be a ruthless path to success and growth.

By backing away from scrutiny, is the reputation of a business and/or its CEO more or less likely to be enhanced or denigrated? Surely the answer is that, in the long term, it will be denigrated. Denying a move towards transparency is ultimately, in our mature Western economies, a Canute-like holding back of the trend of the past 50 years. That qualifying 'long term' is interesting, though, as it does allow in the short term for an advantage to be stolen against competitors, regulators and tax jurisdictions, and even employees and suppliers, by being less than transparent.

The hubristic CEO, particularly our serial chancer as we have outlined above, may choose to play the short game and wield power away from prying eyes in order to secure short-term gains. However, just as we have predicted that, inevitably, the walled gardens erected by the likes of Apple and Amazon will collapse in the long term, so it is that a reputation built on openness and transparency will be the long-term victor over secrecy and covert dealings.

The dilemma of Huawei

At the time of writing, there is a consensus among telecoms tech commentators that Huawei, having already streaked ahead in the past decade to become the world's largest telecoms company, has such a lead in the development of 5G technology that it is in danger of being the only candidate when countries choose the infrastructure required to roll out 5G quickly. Telecom innovators from decades past, Ericsson and Nokia, are playing catch-up, leaving governments with a huge dilemma. Go with Huawei, a cheaper, faster solution but from a secretive and even possibly a secret-stealing, organization intrinsically linked to the Chinese state, or delay the rollout of the huge communications benefits of 5G until an Ericsson/Nokia solution comes along. Several administrations in the US, the UK and in Europe are currently wrestling with this.

The reason for choosing one solution over another, possibly for the first time in relation to a procurement decision this large, is all down to the dominance of this one factor – transparency. Is Huawei sufficiently transparent in its strategy, its motives and its methods for Western powers to entrust their communications platforms to them in the 2020s and beyond?

Technologically, Huawei is clearly brilliant, showing a vision and a level of innovation that has left long-established European providers looking slow and flat-footed. Pricewise and quality-wise, it would appear to provide world-class products at unbeatable prices. In other words, in every other respect, Huawei is hands-down the best available supplier for 5G infrastructure.

And yet it is fighting a constant reputational battle over the clarity of its motives and its purpose. This is, of course, as a result of the interwoven nature of commerce and state in the unique experiment that the Chinese state represents in the capitalist system. Nevertheless, it is an instructive warning to CEOs who favour creating a shield from scrutiny that the taint of an ambiguous motive can be almost impossible to shake off. What a frustration that could be – to have a world-beating combination of an innovative, high-quality product, available at a sector-conquering price, yet with customers reluctant to buy it.

To that end, let Huawei serve as a warning to CEOs tempted to fight against openness and transparency: in the 2020s and beyond, it will be a battle which can only be lost. One can still see the temptation at play in businesses of all sizes; the lure of complete control versus the democratization and accountability brought about by transparency. CEOs must resist the dark side and allow a shining in of the light; as the American lawyer Louis Brandeis said, sunlight is the best disinfectant.

A dismissal of evidence and of consultation

Whether the situation is one of a new CEO in their honeymoon period or an established CEO in charge, a common warning sign of hubristic behaviour is a refusal to take account of evidence put forward or to encourage consultation. Beyond the CEO, but often with them setting the tone and the example, this can take hold at any level in an organization, right down to team leaders not welcoming the views of their teams. At every level it is pride, ambition and a love of status that drives people to suppress the consultative process. Let us look in more detail at the damaging effect this can have on every aspect of a business.

'Fake news'

In public life, facts and the views of experts are under siege. Disinformation and the undermining of the truth can be achieved more easily than ever before via social media and clickbait websites. Of course, the spreading of rumour and false information is as old as civilization itself. Cleopatra helped to propagate the false rumour that she had committed suicide, which led ultimately to Mark Antony killing himself after defeat at the Battle of Actium. While the potentially fatal consequences of playing with the truth are nothing new, the currency of truth has never been more devalued. Even the term 'fake news' has been debased and distorted; it is itself now fake news, too. Trump dismisses all negative coverage, regardless of how accurate or not it may be, as 'fake news' from the 'lamestream media.' As such, we all need to move on and refer to disinformation as something else.

Similarly, in the 2016 Brexit referendum campaign in the UK, various Leave campaigns dismissed facts about the historic benefits of EU membership and the opinions on the likely effect of leaving the EU from business experts and others as either irrelevant or misleading. The Brexit campaign then descended into one fought on slogans and on promises (on both sides of the argument) rather than a reasoned debate that provided the British people with clear information on which to base their decision.

This debasement of experts, of detail, of correlated facts, of the authority of journalism and of the mainstream media has had a cumulative effect, over the past decade or so, of undermining the value of evidence-based actions. In this climate, it can be all too easy for business leaders to feel that they have carte blanche to treat facts and evidence in a similarly cavalier fashion. A poor example has been set from the very top, from politicians in Western democracies, so why not follow that lead?

Gut feeling

Entrepreneurialism has always had to have elements of luck, chance and instinct in order to succeed. The most romanticized wins in corporate history are not the ones where an army of spreadsheet analysts pinpointed the exact optimum moment when a deal should be done, but those which are conducted in exactly the opposite conditions. The impulsive phone call, being in the right place with the right person at the right time, or just 'feeling' that the moment is right. And who would want to crush those serendipitous events? They are moments of magic which people remember (and are remembered for) for the rest of their careers.

The problem is that for each one of these rare events, things don't always turn out that way. More often than not it is the wrong place with the wrong person at the wrong time. Strangely, these are the examples which don't make it into the tycoon's colourful autobiography or 'how to' book. But, having read a few such books, our ambitious CEO, who has always fancied himself as a clever salesperson, decides to make a headline-grabbing deal. This could be yet another example of our new CEO being desperate to demonstrate some 'thinking outside the box' that the established board has been too dim-witted and blinkered to spot. Or it could a long-incumbent CEO turning attention on a

Too Proud to Lead

new market or territory for no good reason other than boredom and overfamiliarity with existing markets. Either way, the leap in the dark is not much more than that: a leap of faith with no solid analysis behind it, with often fatal consequences.

One plus one never equals three

Of all the corporate buzzwords of the past few decades, the one which has promised so much and delivered so little is 'synergy'. Fifty years of failed or failing mergers and acquisitions and still nothing seems to have been learned. In nine out of ten cases, it is the acquired business that benefits more than the acquirer, which is surely the wrong way around. Why pay money for an ailing or failing business, throwing it a lifeline, only for it to be a massive distraction from the primary focus of your business? Buying up a competitor is ultimately not a display of strength but a sign of weakness. You can't beat it on the consumer battlefield, so you just dig out the chequebook and pay for the battle to end. And, time and again, acquiring businesses, even in the same sector, or perhaps especially in the same sector, fails as a result of cultural mismatches. The 'culture' of the business is missing from the spreadsheets, if such a thing as culture is even looked at. It is hard to define it as the 'way we do things'; you cannot get under the skin of an organization until you are in there, too late, *after* the acquisition.

'This acquisition will create a synergy between our businesses, making it bigger and better than the sum of the parts.' How often have we heard that claim in our corporate lives? And how often does hindsight prove a wonderful thing? In the world of mergers and acquisitions, one plus one never equals three. And in the intervening couple of years, the parent company's attention has been focused on its new problem child instead of where it should be directed – on customers, markets, supplier relationships and, above all, the motivation and welfare of its employees.

Organic growth versus acquisition

We are focusing on mergers and acquisitions because they have produced such vivid examples of CEO gut-feeling, impulsiveness and hubris. They are a reduction of shrewd commerce to nothing more than a game of Monopoly, too often landing on *Chance* and even occasionally on *Go to Jail* rather than an expensive property. The successful giants we discussed earlier, such as Facebook and Apple, have an acquisitions history that is a mixture of the shrewd, the failed and the ultimately irrelevant. Their pockets have been deep enough that a 'win-some, lose-some' approach has had few downsides for them. This is not the case for most businesses, however, where one or two significant acquisitions are the only chances they have to get it right. It is perhaps telling, as we outlined in the Bezos case study, that one of Amazon's key strengths has been its strategy of building outwards using existing expertise, as shown by its scaling up via Marketplace, Amazon Web Services and its AI division. Logical, organic growth beats wayward culture-shock acquisition nearly every time. It's not a sexy quick win, but it's often a 'tortoise beats hare' outcome.

Examples of acquisition failure

The dotcom bubble of the late 1990s paved the way for all rational thought to be discarded in the acquisition game. It became a mad land grab of any half-decent idea wrapped up in some lossmaking venture. 'If it's losing money it must be good' became the *Alice Through the Looking Glass* reasoning of the venture capitalists. It was a frenzied period, and FOMO on a massive scale. Yet Fear Of Missing Out never makes for good conditions under which to make rational business decisions. It's like grabbing a bargain on Black Friday; when you get it home, buyer's remorse can quickly set in.

Here are a couple of acquisition examples from long after the dotcom bubble had burst which show that these same mistakes can still be made. Both examples are strongly identified as being driven by the impulse of the CEO at the time, which is why we are using them here as cautionary tales. You can see the psychology at work, imagine the eye-rolling and shoulder shrugging in the boardroom as the irrationality of the plan became clear, and then sense the feeling of powerlessness as it was implemented. In the second case, it resulted in the hastened departure of the CEO; in the first it was just something to be moved on from and never spoken of again.

Murdoch acquires Myspace

It's 2006 and Rupert Murdoch is 74 years old. He's the most powerful media mogul in the world and has decided that it's time to get down with the kids and move into the new channel of social media. Just before Facebook gets going properly, Myspace is the most popular social media site, so Murdoch's News Corporation buys it for $580 million. Murdoch has had a long and remarkable business career and, at the time of writing, is still going strong at 90 years old. He may well represent the last of his kind: an old-style dynastic leader, a Hearst/Kane figure who has lasted well into the twenty-first century. So what happened next is but a mere blip in an incredibly impressive career, but it remains an instructive one.

In the heady days of 2006, Myspace is the most visited website in the US, at the time even outranking Google. For the first couple of years, it looks to be yet another shrewd Murdoch move, with a valuation on paper (whatever that means with this type of business) for Myspace of $12 billion. Unfortunately for Murdoch and News Corp, this is as good as it gets, and things start to unravel fast. When faced with a competitor as exceptional as Facebook, maybe that is not surprising, but it is the hubristic nature of a couple of decisions that is instructive in this saga.

Fast-forward five years to 2011 and News Corp sells Myspace for an undisclosed sum, but is thought to be as little as $35 million. Casting ahead, that loss of over $500 million is small change compared to the opportunity lost of not being a primary mover in social media, which of course would now be worth billions. So, what went wrong? The main reason the acquisition failed is that Murdoch decided to bend Myspace into, if you will, His-space, yet another Murdoch entertainment channel. It's a classic example of a CEO making decisions which reflect their biases, their background and retreating into their comfort zone. Murdoch understands monetizing content and beaming news and entertainment into people's homes, a core strength of the News Corp empire to this day.

Instead of being a platform for sharing and interacting, Myspace becomes a music and entertainment portal, something the fledgling YouTube will soon overshadow in its reach and usability. Murdoch saw it as a distribution outlet for his own Fox studio content, completely missing the point of its purpose as a social media platform for others to upload content.

Myspace's limited usability and styling is where the second mistake was made. Myspace retained all development control by keeping it in-house, just at the time that Facebook created a platform for any external developer to build new applications. For an old-school controlling mogul like Murdoch, that whole open and hive-mind concept would have been totally alien. As a result, the design, functionality and cool halo of Facebook (at that time) soon accelerated rapidly past Myspace and the rest is history.

Murdoch has apparently referred to purchasing Myspace as a 'huge mistake', which illustrates further just how adrift his thinking is on this whole episode. To him, he was unable to reshape Myspace in his own image and make it successful. Purchasing Myspace in 2006 was not a mistake. On the contrary, it was potentially the biggest stroke of genius in his entire illustrious career, purchased right on the cusp of when social media was to go stratospheric. With the right approach and an open and creative mindset, it could have launched a whole new media stream, just as Murdoch had done with satellite TV in the UK. The journey since speaks for itself: News Corp has a current valuation of around $9 billion, while Facebook is worth in excess of $500 billion.

Here is an owner, spotting a golden chance and then blowing it, by thinking that he knows better than the market about what the market wants. This has worked in the past, so it can surely work again. This is a falling back on track record which ends up in what could arguably be classified as the biggest lost opportunity in the history of commerce. *That is a tough price to pay for a proud and hubristic approach to a new market, but a cautionary tale worth noting.*

We have already referenced the 2010 movie *The Social Network* in our case study of Mark Zuckerberg. A lovely postscript to the Myspace story is that the purchaser of Myspace for such a small sum in 2011 was a company called Specific Media. One of the people with a stake in this deal was the singer and actor Justin Timberlake, who at the time of the acquisition of Myspace was declared by Specific Media CEO Tim Vangerhook as the person who would 'lead the business strategy' as it moved forward. So, a year after playing Facebook investor Sean Parker, Timberlake clearly fancied a shot at this sort of Svengali role for real. While Parker's prescient early slice of Facebook has placed him on the *Forbes* magazine list of the world's wealthiest people, Justin Timberlake has remained well advised to continue his successful singing and acting career, as a diversion into social media entrepreneurship has not led anywhere. Myspace was sold on to Time Inc. in 2016, albeit at a modest profit.

Microsoft acquires Nokia

Our second example of a misguided acquisition and what it says about the mindset of a hubristic CEO is the sorry tale of Microsoft's acquisition of Nokia in 2014 for $7.9 billion. The stakes here in acquisition cost terms were higher, although in the greater scheme of things have not proved to be a major issue for Microsoft. For Microsoft CEO Steve Ballmer, however, the deal proved to be the end of the line.

However, it is an illuminating tale in that it displays a vaulting ambition at work that was out of touch with reality. When you are the CEO of the world's dominant software company it may well be tempting to believe you can be successful in other areas, too. The genius of Bill Gates was to understand, from the outset, that software was the route to every desktop and workspace in the world, not hardware. By single-mindedly focusing on an operating system, Windows, and a mainstream software application which could be used by every office worker, Office, he went on to conquer the world.

Steve Ballmer joined Microsoft in 1980 as the first business manager hired by Gates. By 2013/14, he had nearly 35 years' experience of understanding the power of Gates' idea. He had also, since taking over as CEO of Microsoft in 2000, presided over a dozen years of a series of low-key attempts to enter the tech hardware market, producing a number of also-ran devices. In entertainment, portable computing and phones, Microsoft had let Apple and Google's Android dominate that part of the operating system market.

None of that prevented Ballmer from one final high stakes throw of the dice. The smartphone boat had sailed back in 2007 with the launch of Apple's iPhone, with those intervening six years constituting dog years in the fast-moving world of portable consumer tech. Google's Android operating system was launched a year later, in 2008.

A major casualty of these two initiatives was the Finnish company squeezed in the middle, Nokia, which had dominated mobile telecoms for the best part of the two decades leading up to the launch of the iPhone.

By 2013, Nokia was, to all intents and purposes, dead and buried. Imagine their surprise and delight when Steve Ballmer throws them his ill-advised multi-billion-dollar lifeline. What a short-lived marriage made in hell it proved to be, for both parties. Nokia had entered into a 'strategic partnership' with Microsoft in 2011, adopting its Windows Phone operating system instead of Android. This did little to improve Nokia's fortunes and analysts believe that Ballmer's decision to purchase

Nokia was because the Finnish company was close to abandoning Windows in favour of Android, leaving Microsoft with no significant hardware platform for its phone operating system. The acquisition of Nokia was Ballmer's last significant move as CEO and he stepped down in February 2014, with the purchased assets of Nokia written off by Microsoft in 2015.

So, Ballmer had set himself and Microsoft the equivalent challenge of pushing two streams of water uphill at the same time. With a dismal track record in hardware sales and innovation, they took on the dual role of major smartphone manufacturer and distributor. And to do so, they chose a phone brand which, in the minds of consumers, was stranded in a previous decade. First-mover advantage has served Microsoft well in computer operating systems. Be installed first in every major manufacturers' hardware and get every office worker familiar and happy with your software and nothing can stop that momentum.

However, try to enter hardware and software markets years late when you are the nth player in a market dominated by two savvy players (Apple and Google), and where is that going to get you? Nowhere. You don't need to be a business school graduate to work that one out, but Ballmer's belief that Microsoft's power and dominance in one sector would carry across into others is a classic display of hubris and misplaced pride.

The beautifully idiosyncratic and idealistic philosophy of Nokia which powered this unlikely business to phenomenal success, makes their demise at the hands of Ballmer all the more poignant. If he threw them some sort of misguided lifeline, it somehow made the final ignominy even worse.

Listen to reason

Both the Myspace/News Corp story and the Nokia/Microsoft tale highlight the vanity lurking behind many mergers and acquisitions.

We have personalized them as Murdoch and Ballmer case studies because in both examples there is plenty of evidence from comments at the time and subsequent analysis that as heads of their respective businesses they have taken direct responsibility and ownership of the decisions made.

Mergers and acquisitions have been a growth industry in themselves in the past 30–40 years. The fastest growing part of commercial law in that period has been in that area, with all the major law firms offering crack teams to steer companies through the intricacies of acquisition in the face of increased monopolistic scrutiny. As we have seen from these examples (and there are dozens of other high-profile cases we could have chosen), these are moments in a company's progress – particularly in relation to buy-outs, acquisitions and takeovers – when the ambition, the limits of expertise and the over-reliance on the gut instinct of a CEO can have catastrophic consequences. There may well have been voices of reason suggesting ways to avoid the mistakes made, but here, as in many other boardrooms in similar situations, reason can often be drowned out by the hubris of a powerful, overconfident, lone voice.

A failure to reach out

It's now time to explore a different aspect of hubristic leadership, one that involves a shutting down of debate or of the opportunities provided by collaboration. Collaboration is not only restricted to within a company; it also applies to the willingness to seeking input from a range of external stakeholders. Whether collaborated efforts are internal or external, the outcomes are similar when they are discouraged. To shut down a more sharing and inclusive approach results in a blinkered vision and limits future possibilities. The merits of collaboration, in all its various guises, are key components in slaying hubris and are discussed later in the book. In this section, however, the dangers of failing to take an open and collaborative approach are highlighted.

You cannot know everything

The pressures from all sides, the pace of change in every sector, the constant need for renewal, reinvention and re-evaluation (multiplied exponentially, of course, in the light of the coronavirus pandemic) – all of these mean that decision-making is more complex for CEOs than ever before. It requires more knowledge, more data, and more understanding than in past decades and yet CEOs seem to fall into two distinct decision-making camps.

There are those who feel that, because so much needs to be known in order to make the best possible decisions, they are the only ones who can understand all the complexities. Instead of acknowledging the need for a multi-faceted approach, viewed from all angles, an arrogance kicks in which denies the input of others. Just when it is most needed, the stance is taken that only a single, clear vision, unencumbered by conflicting arguments, can steer the business in a decisive direction.

As we have seen, there is an elite band of leaders who have succeeded with this approach. Jobs, Zuckerberg, Bezos and Musk all qualify as leaders whose strength of vision and original thought have powered them and their organizations to pre-eminence. As we have also noted, though, this has often come at a heavy price, with payback likely due at some point.

For the rest of us mere mortals, any attempts to emulate such boldness and single-mindedness should be approached with extreme caution. We have already seen how easy it is to get things catastrophically wrong, as the Murdoch/Myspace and Ballmer/Nokia episodes illustrate. And yet we still see CEOs displaying behaviour which favours fast, uninformed decisions rather than slower, more considered approaches.

The tyranny of the reporting cycle, as we've mentioned, is a key driver of short-termism and produces a compulsion to release announcements quickly. That perceived impatience with the markets is, however, more an excuse for steamrollering through a seat-of-the-pants decision than a reality. In fact, most markets yearn for evidence of planning, of a coherent strategy supported by some consistency of vision. If the research, logic and reasoning is not available to support a new initiative, then however bold, radical and original it is, if the detailed rationale is not available in a follow-up briefing to fund managers, the whole thing is in danger of being picked apart.

Study the evidence

Bold, radical and original are so much more headline-grabbing than solid, carefully researched and logical, and to achieve this latter version requires active collaboration and reasoned debate. It requires admitting that you may not have all the answers straight off the bat. You've had to be curious, be willing to seek advice from specialists in their field, from people who work for you who, in their own way, know more than you do about their specific area. It is about recognizing that you don't in fact need to be the smartest person in the room, because it is likely that there are others who will know more about a market sector, a geographic market, a manufacturing technique, an IT solution – a million and one other things – than you do.

There are still CEOs out there who can't admit that they know less than others. These are the sort of people who, in the face of a detailed objection to a point of policy or strategy, fire back with: 'You're not looking at the bigger picture.' A core part of the CEO's role is, of course, to do just that, to look wider and further, endeavouring to look over the horizon in a way that more functional board members are less inclined to. But there needs to be a balance, a skilled appreciation of minutiae as well as of the more broad-brush considerations. There is a need to be humble in the face of facts, data and evidence. It is the responsibility of the CEO's team to present such detail in a way that makes its assimilation and analysis as easy as possible, without dumbing it down. Then, if that is done, it is up to the CEO to have the humility to appreciate the additional insight and knowledge which has been presented and to act upon its findings.

The political responses to the challenges of the coronavirus pandemic displayed interesting approaches to the importance of evidence, in this case scientific and medical. The UK government claimed to be making decisions 'based on the best science and evidence'. However, this is in danger of becoming a shield behind which politicians can hide, abdicating responsibility for decision-making. The 'experts', instead of being listened to and then decisions being made based on their guidance and evidence, are potentially being set up to take the blame if things go wrong.

In the business world, decisions and the interpretation of evidence are never as high stakes in terms of the effects on millions of people's lives as the current pandemic, but the syndrome described is another distorting way in which an ambitious CEO can choose to treat advisers. Rather than ignoring evidence and advice, this can sometimes be adopted too literally, unencumbered by the unique CEO perspective and often with the preface 'Upon the advice of my team, I have decided to ...' in a way that is designed to spread blame or responsibility. CEOs should own their decisions and responsibilities, not abdicate them.

Signs of a lack of respect for evidence, for experts and for facts-based advice, can be clear warning signs of hubris and buck-passing. Being sufficiently self-aware to admit that you don't know everything can come hard to the ambitious business leader, but doing so will only engender more respect, not less.

Rewarding corporate swagger

We still live in a business culture that rewards confidence, entrepreneurial risk-taking (when it lands the deal) and the survival of the fittest. The phrase 'a cautious approach' is nearly always couched in derogatory terms, expressing scorn for the slow performer about to be outsmarted by a more aggressive rival. In this environment the line between confidence and arrogance can be a fine one, and spotting it, curbing it, indeed channelling it in the right direction, can be hard.

Indeed, the slide into hubristic tendencies is, as we have shown, all too easily achieved. It is not difficult to see how confidence might grow as success continues to follow you: why it would seem reasonable to conclude that past successes are the winning formula for future success; why your judgement and decision-making are by far the best, based on the judgement calls you made that went against the grain but which were, in the end, proved right. On their own, it's easy to put forward an argument that these are winning strategies for successful leadership, yet, like most things, it is only when you look deeper into them that you can see a level of interconnectedness that can have damaging consequences. The potential for outstanding leadership lies in recognizing that susceptibility to hubris is far more common than you may think.

In the next part of this book we focus on what leaders can do to guard against falling into the hubris trap. If you are a CEO (or an aspiring one), you need to recognize that it may take some discipline, that ultimately it is about having the ability to harness those practices and behaviours that build dynamic organizations, and instil them with purpose. And those organizations are usually guided by leaders who seek to create something bigger and better than themselves. It is to this that we now turn our attention in the upcoming chapters.

PART 2

CHAPTER 6

Balancing Collaboration with Urgency

Start listening

We have observed the pitfalls of a hubristic style of management across various high-profile organizations. We have seen that a culture of secrecy, denial and fear has pervaded those businesses that have ultimately been wholly or partially undone by the choices and actions of their decision-makers. This has certainly been true at Boeing (with tragic consequences), as well as at WeWork, Uber, General Motors and Deutsche Bank. Whistleblowers were silenced, departmental experts were ignored, and external scrutiny was suppressed.

In the light of these stories, what could have been done differently to avoid the catastrophic outcomes we have documented? A good starting point would have been to place organizational ahead of individual achievement. The reckless, self-aggrandizing behaviour of hubristic leaders could have been counter-balanced with more reasoned, considered strategies if other voices had been heard and other viewpoints had been allowed into the decision-making process. By focusing on the desire to be recognized as bold, audacious and innovative, some of the hubristic leaders we have profiled donned self-imposed blinkers which prevented them from seeing the bigger picture and considering the longer-term implications of their strategies and actions. These were high-stakes games, culminating in a stark choice between going out in a blaze of glory or crashing and burning.

The reason these leaders followed their chosen path was because, as well as fuelling their egos, it represented the easier route. That may sound counter-intuitive. Going out on a limb, having the courage to single-mindedly run with a bold idea or to tough out a difficult situation, is surely the harder thing to do? In some ways, of course, that's true; on balance, however, it is consultation and collaboration which is the harder way of doing things.

Collaboration is hard

Collaboration requires more patience, more listening, more open-mindedness, more humility and more willingness to share power and responsibility. Steamroller through a policy, a strategy or a set of tactics and the CEO's mandate can be accomplished by pronouncing it in a meeting, or by sending a broadcast email. Enter into a collaborative or co-operative approach and a huge number of extra stages and dimensions come into play. Data needs to be gathered and analysed. Detailed planning of resources and project management needs to be put in place. Consultation with a wide range of stakeholders needs to be set up with every relevant stakeholder: departmental experts, customers, suppliers, even regulators and government, depending upon the nature of the project.

For the average CEO, their bold initiative is now mired in delay, in weighing up evidence and evaluating opposing arguments, in making an effort to focus on detail, in, horror of horrors, modifying the original idea in the light of a convincing argument. This means having the humility to accept that your ideas may not have been perfect in the first place.

We have already explored how dogmatic and dangerous the 'Never explain, never complain' mantra can be, and a collaborative approach means going back on both of those 'nevers'. And that means adopting a humble, inclusive approach, one that often sits uneasily on the shoulders of CEOs who have fought their way to the top precisely by being driven and single-minded.

Balancing time versus risk

This wider, more considered form of leadership requires skills that are different to those of an old-school, buccaneering entrepreneur. The key new skill is mastering the trick of remaining nimble while at the same time allowing considerable additional input into the decision-making processes. It's about balancing the risk of imposing an inevitable delay on the system for implementation against the benefit of reaching a more rounded, informed decision. It becomes a matter of moving from one three-step process:

1. Idea or problem
2. Reliance on past for identifying solution
3. Execute

to another:

1. Problem or idea
2. Explore; research, discuss, test
3. Execute and refine

The first three-step process reflects a confidence and belief, substantiated by past results, that causes you to believe that the answer lies with you alone, and/or that simply replicating the same strategy will yield equal success this time around. After all, didn't it work before? This inclination to attribute successes primarily to your own actions may come naturally to a leader; actions and success provide a clear and linear connection between the two, but the reality is that this can be a dangerous course of action to rely on.

In the second example of a three-step process, it is step two where the key difference lies. Instead of relying on the past, or becoming wrapped up in their own success, leaders pursue the course of using discovery as a means to form their views. A quest to seek out alternative views, pursue new perspectives, search for diverse opinions: all are used to inform the ultimate decision. Of course, these extra processes of discussion, researching, testing and refining prior to implementation can take the project/strategy in two possible directions. The danger is that they can fatally slow down decision-making, dilute, confuse and compromise the strength of the original idea. The flip side is that a good idea becomes a great idea, one that is truly ahead of the competition and has a sustainable life within the business because it is now owned by all relevant stakeholders.

Our CEO now needs to earn the reward package. It turns out that collaboration and co-operation are not about abdicating responsibility; they are about marshalling diverse views and opinions, and weaving a consensus which achieves the perfect balance of timeliness, coherence and clarity. By retaining those qualities within the original idea, the CEO achieves the best of both worlds: boldness of vision matched by the broadest consensus and buy-in.

In a section below relating to the relationship between perfection and progress, we will see that the complexity implicit in achieving that is multiplied further by taking on board a broader purpose than profit and shareholder value, adding a whole extra range of considerations against which the idea is evaluated. More on that later.

'Perfection is the enemy of progress'

This is another Churchill quote, and one that gets to the heart of the CEO's conundrum. More listening, more analysis, more research and testing can end up being a series of reasons to hesitate, to dilute, to compromise and, ultimately, to fatally delay. Office walls are adorned with annoyingly glib motivational quotes featuring striving athletes, and this one from Mark Twain is sometimes among them: 'The secret of getting ahead is getting started.'

The quote continues: 'The secret of getting started is breaking your complex overwhelming tasks into small manageable tasks, and then starting on the first one.'

This is sound advice, and the key role now for the CEO is to a) ensure things get started, and b) enable 'complex and overwhelming' to be turned into 'small and manageable'.

It is the skilled CEO who finds the sweet spot between thought and action, and between involvement and decision. For the CEO who relishes control, this increases rather than diminishes it. Instead of controlling a simple set of linear commands, we're now conducting an entire orchestra, controlling a wide range of causes and effects to end up with music and harmony.

All this is difficult and potentially stressful, which is why so many CEOs prefer the shortcut of 'getting started' rather than the next bit, which is often in smaller print on that motivational poster. Any forward motion is seen as better than none at all, any 'initiative' is invaluable for filling that blank page on the shareholder update. Be bold and decisive, and worry about the consequences later. This action-at-all-costs is part of the short-termism we were cursing earlier, and often results in announcements that are more style than substance and end up disengaging stakeholders, as they had not been involved in the 'initiative' or were possibly unaware of its very existence.

Together we win

Far better, even with all the caveats of the benefits of just 'getting started' and of avoiding seeking perfection before making progress, is a more inclusive and consultative approach. The CEO who reaches out and recognizes that he/she does not have all the answers will be the one who becomes the biggest winner. The better mindset is to take pride in a collective win, not to take credit for an individual success. How much more fun to have a boardroom celebration that involves everyone for a strategic win, where every C-suite member can genuinely feel they have made a contribution towards it compared with the CEO receiving a series of one-way emails from board members, dutifully congratulating oh mighty leader on an amazing triumph.

How to get to that celebratory moment, and to make it an event that is not just a one-off, but one that can occur regularly? The best and most logical starting point is for the CEO to assemble a strong, dynamic, motivated and resourceful board or C-suite and to leverage the talents of people within and outside the organization.

The CEO and the board balance

Let's go back to basics for a moment. What is the definition of a CEO's role? You could if, you wished, look no further than Investopedia, which defines the role in this way:

> 'A chief executive officer (CEO) is the highest-ranking executive in a company, whose primary responsibilities include making major corporate decisions, managing the overall operations and resources of a company, acting as the main point of communication between the board of directors (the board) and corporate operations and being the public face of the company. A CEO is elected by the board and its shareholders.'

Whether it's a conclusive definition or one that is based on your own observations and experiences, or comes from reading about leadership, it's broadly agreed that the position of CEO carries immense power and responsibility. This last point is easy to forget. Ultimately, a CEO is accountable to the board and the company's shareholders, not, as sometimes seems to be the case, the other way around. The domineering, dictatorial CEO can be pushed out and perhaps a few boards need to remind themselves of that fact occasionally.

However, let us consider a more constructive path, one where the CEO and the board work in constructive harmony. This board needs to be as honest and as open as our model CEO, or any ambitions of collaboration and co-operation will come to a juddering halt at the exit to the boardroom. The board should be the team that helps guide the development and implementation of strategy, with a style of management, communication and collaboration that creates the best possible balance between careful consideration of a strategy and the speed of its implementation.

The CEO needs to share power, responsibility, perspective and implementation with the board. If the optimum co-operative and collaborative conditions can be created for this grouping, then similarly high levels of collaborative activity will cascade down through the organization.

It becomes all about leading by example. A C-suite which is seen by employees at all levels to be working in harmony and with a clear common purpose encourages everyone to discard rivalries, politics, gossip and self-interest, and focus instead on the true goal of enhancing the value and purpose of the business. If co-operation between functions is optimized, then the vital speed of clear decision-making is accelerated. Factionalism slows everything down but acting in a co-ordinated manner on a strategy or project will only ever speed things up.

The communication balances

In the cascade from a strategy or project implementation, if there is clarity at the outset about objectives, budgets, timescales, expectations and objectives, then – guess what – people will buy into it more quickly. Inter-disciplinary and inter-departmental briefings and teams will break down barriers to that communication. Enabling an ethos where all of that can take place, regardless of the origins of a specific project, will be where teams can perform at their best. Leaders who are able to co-ordinate all the elements and functions and can assemble the perfect blend of talents for each project – this is where their primary contribution to the speed and efficiency of a good outcome will lie. Get it right and the project will fly, the optimum pooling of talent creating a faster, smarter outcome.

The challenge, however, is that 'communicating', 'briefing' and 'collaborative working' are all terms which, if not handled subtly and carefully, bring to mind processes that simply slow down and hinder the implementation of a project, rather than contributing to the vital speed needed. *'Talking'* about the best ways to structure and implement a project is one step back from going ahead and implementing it.

'We know what needs doing. Can't we just get on with it?' If the answer to such plain speaking is continuing talk of process rather than action, it's highly likely that the audience has been lost and probably the patience of the CEO, too. At that point, co-operation and collaboration becomes a devalued concept in the eyes of teams across the business and the next time anyone tries it, it will probably be greeted (possibly correctly) with boredom and cynicism. As such, it is vital to ensure that the culture of an organization facilitates effective ways in which engagement and involvement are interlinked with accountability.

The co-operation balance

It's probably no exaggeration to state that as the process of getting collaboration and co-operation right becomes harder to pay attention to, the more successful a CEO becomes. The trick is to ensure that the right checks and balances are in place, which remove internal competition for budgets, status and resources, while still remaining commercially sharp. It is about creating nimble means of engagement and participation, which in turn lead to better solutions to issues but not to the detriment of urgency and speed. A more inclusive approach must be seen to work first time around, or it will be abandoned in the face of a commercial setback triggered by a slow response.

The competitive balance

External competition is always the driving force behind any business, forcing it to constantly examine ways to innovate and seek to develop new strategies, products, services and ideas. Competition keeps all businesses sharp, particularly when there are no longer any guarantees of corporate survival. Brands that once seemed to be a permanent part of the commercial landscape have disappeared. Conversely, none of the top five largest companies in the world by market capitalization – Saudi Aramco, Apple, Microsoft, Amazon and Alphabet (Google) – existed before 1975. The corporate landscape is in a constant state of flux, and that was even before the ongoing seismic shake-up created by the coronavirus pandemic. In the light of all that, staying sharp, alert and responsive is critical.

Create too safe and collegiate an environment internally, with too much emphasis on team building and involvement, and impetus and urgency suffer. But fail to consult or to tap into ideas and solutions from across the business and you are back to relying on the CEO's gut instincts for your strategy. It's a delicate balancing act! Pull off the trick of being consultative and collaborative internally, as well as with customers, suppliers and other stakeholders, in order to create a strategy with maximum buy-in and roundedness of thought *and* achieve all that with no discernible reaction time lag, and you are on to a winning formula.

Be competitive outwardly, non-competitive inwardly

If such a balanced environment can be created, the CEO has no choice but to be a team player; the opportunity for hubris has simply been blocked. Instead, a culture has been created that is the best of both worlds: sharp, urgent and entrepreneurial out in the marketplace; collaborative, consultative and non-competing internally. If the CEO has created this culture, any U-turn will demand an explanation. If the CEO has merely bought into it, then the C-suite needs to remain vigilant about the level of buy-in and keep testing it.

Time: the most precious commodity

If the right culture has been created, the benefits will start to speak for themselves: better quality decisions, benefiting from more detailed and rounded information; vastly increased morale and motivation across employees, suppliers and even customers, who start to feel more valued and listened to. The critical measurement is not cost, but time (although one, of course, leads to the other: time is, after all, money). Time can never be regained – once it's gone, it's gone. It's the one commodity that every business has in equal measure. Every trade-off of time in exchange for wider involvement *must* be justified. By highlighting 'time' as the most precious commodity, you impose focus and momentum on to every project, strategy or tactic.

However, this is not the end of the process. There is a whole extra layer of challenge and complexity in the policy- and strategy-forming process which we have not yet added to the mix. As we enter the third decade of the twenty-first century, it is clearer than ever that the checklist of considerations to be taken into account when framing policy and strategy is growing.

For any responsible organization, profit and shareholder value are no longer enough. These certainly need to remain at the heart of any business that relies on making a profit for its continued survival. But longer-term survival now depends on a broader range of criteria being fulfilled. Today's stakeholders in a business – its employees, its suppliers and its customers – are demanding more. They are looking for clear signs of the values and purpose that underpin the business.

Cultivate shared values and a common purpose

So if the decision-making process and strategy formulation have been broadened as a result of greater collaboration and co-operation, they now need to be developed further. Companies concerned with legacy, relevance and long-term survival are doing just this. There is a need to develop a value- and purpose-driven vision for the future. By doing so, organizations are democratizing their purpose, creating ownership of it throughout the business. Ethical, equitable, environmental and societal values now need to be embraced. This becomes a shared, multi-faceted vision, far removed from being a top-down, balance-sheet focused strategy. By adopting a shared rather than a CEO-driven vision, companies will prevent most of the risks of a skewed, hubristic approach taking root.

This is a healthy development and one that we should all embrace. Collaboration and co-operation become not just a means to an end but are part of the purpose of an organization. Reaching out and involving communities on a local, regional or even a national level, depending on the scale and reach of the business, becomes part of the transactional purpose of the business. Community initiatives, charitable alliances, loyalty reward programmes and profit-sharing schemes are all examples of ways in which a business opens its doors more widely to employees, their families and other stakeholders.

The environmental impact of every choice a business makes is now, more than ever, under scrutiny. Energy use, recycling rates, investment choices, sourcing decisions, the carbon footprint of a product or service's lifecycle and many other factors are all now under the spotlight.

In the world today, any CEO concerned about the perception of their business in relation to its community image and its environmental credentials will be broadening their outlook and their vision to consider how they are contributing to society at large. To run an honest, open and ethical business, you need an honest, open and ethical outlook. This may be stating the obvious, but for many

CEOs who perhaps cut their business teeth in the 1980s or even the 1990s, this may require a reappraisal and a recalibration of values and outlook.

The onset of the Covid-19 crisis in early 2020 put the spotlight on companies and CEOs and how purpose is embedded into the fabric of their organizations. You can game the system and develop PR gloss and spin to paper over the gaps between intention and deeds for a certain amount of time, but in the end that gap will be exposed and you will be found out. The strain of saying one thing and doing another takes its toll, and in this age of democratizing social media and whistleblowing, hypocrisy and mere lip service to causes are being exposed. The modern CEO needs to lead by example, demonstrating values and ethics which 20 years ago they would never have been questioned about. Things are changing and CEOs need to change, too.

This wider agenda of accountability that now sits on CEOs' shoulders helps to militate against a cultivation of hubris. Pride in success can now only truly be achieved when a wide range of benchmarks are in place; to ensure long-term success, it is no longer enough just to be a profitable business. The way in which those profits are achieved is rightly under the microscope, and for a CEO to leave a genuine legacy they must satisfy a range of ethical and moral as well as commercial standards.

Transparency, accountability, fairness and a demonstrable set of values – these should all now be paramount in any self-respecting CEO's frame of reference when considering their conduct and their vision for their business. Such qualities suppress their hubristic opposites: a self-serving agenda, secrecy and narrow-mindedness.

The CEO success timeline

In this chapter we have established that the enemy of hubris is collaboration. We have also seen that collaboration has to be balanced against time, the ticking clock of the constant need for urgency to keep moving the business forward. And that the collaborative process has, in the last 20 years or so, become the subject of a wider agenda – that of working towards shared values and purpose.

In the next chapter we'll look at a different consideration of time: the timeline of a CEO's progress within a particular organization and the hubris pressure points and warning signs along that progression.

CHAPTER 7

The CEO Hubris Timeline

There is a universality that may be traced in the career arc of a CEO within an organization, a common and detectable narrative that is worth analysing in order to highlight exactly where the hubris pressure points lie. By doing this, we can all be extra vigilant in recognizing when they occur and develop strategies for snuffing them out. We have touched on some of these earlier and recognized others in the case studies, but by looking at them as a narrative timeline it may help to see the issues more clearly.

Inevitably, there is a degree of generalization here: for each syndrome we outline, there will be many CEOs who act completely differently from the way we are commenting. However, having observed the workings of businesses across a wide range of sectors, countries and cultures, we have discovered a remarkable commonality of behaviour exhibited by CEOs in similar phases of their tenure within organizations.

Broadly, there are three phases:

1. **Horizon one.** The learner – new leader: the honeymoon period, as we described it earlier. This can be anything up to the first 18 months of a CEO's initial tenure, although it can also come to an abrupt end after a mere three months. This very much depends on events and on the timing of the appointment in relation to the business's reporting cycle.
2. **Horizon two.** The successful CEO – consolidating power: after the honeymoon comes perhaps the optimum period in which a CEO makes their mark and makes a difference. It is also, attitudinally,

the riskiest phase, one which can go either way in terms of pride or humility, collaboration or hubris. This can be any time up to the first three to five years of activity.

3. **Horizon three.** The danger zone: the confident, established leader. Having settled into the role and with a series of successes behind him (and maybe some failures, too, along the way), our leader is now sitting more comfortably in the role, perhaps a little too comfortably …

The management dynamic, the attitude to success, the level of inclusiveness and collaboration, and ultimately the level of humility demonstrated – all these factors and more can shift and change during these three phases. Let's examine each phase in more detail and highlight the points of danger along the way.

Horizon one: the learner

New leader phase: making their mark

New CEOs are appointed in any number of different circumstances, depending on the manner of the departure of the outgoing incumbent. A leader at the top of their game decides to call it a day, with the company at an apex of achievement, and thus an opportunity arises for a new CEO-ship. Conversely, it could be on the back of an unceremonious firing of the CEO, following commercial disaster or a financial scandal. Whatever the reason for the arrival of a new CEO, the event will trigger high hopes and expectations. Whether it's just new blood being pumped into the leadership of the organization, or the appointment of someone – anyone – to salvage a corporate reputation in tatters, all stakeholders in the business will be studying this first phase with a sense of anticipation and optimism.

Likewise, the new CEO will see this as a new start, a fresh chapter and an exciting new challenge. Accepting the job of CEO is not one that anyone should take on lightly or feel complacent and comfortable about on their first day. Even for the most seasoned practitioner, with an impressive CV and previous CEO-ships under their belt, it is a role that carries a significant responsibility and accountability. The livelihoods of employees and their families lie in their hands, along with potentially many others who rely on that business – suppliers, investors, the economy local to that business, a whole set of concentric circles spreading out from the wealth creation on which that business rests. It's a grave responsibility, and one which the old adage 'the buck stops here' continues to sum up perfectly.

It doesn't matter whether it's a dozen, hundreds, thousands or even hundreds of thousands of people who are dependent on your company for their futures: the importance of the CEO's role is the same to all of those who sit beneath it. Any CEO would do well to bear that in mind.

Assuming there is an awareness and understanding of the significance of the role by the new leader, what are their likely first moves and early attitudes to the role?

New leader phase: be a vision creator

In the early days, leaders seek to set out their stall. As a leader, you are fully aware that all eyes are on you. Who are you? What do you stand for? Now, more than ever, it is incumbent on leaders to paint a vivid picture of what's possible, to engage and motivate people to see what the future holds and the part that they play in creating this future. It is at this early stage that people will scrutinize 'how a leader shows up'. Equally, it is the time when leaders are most likely to conduct themselves with honesty and authenticity; when they should be focused on bringing people with them on a journey where everyday successes matter, too. Passion converts people to a cause, and the passion of a CEO can come from many places: for example, a deep-seated desire for approval; or a yearning to create something bigger, better and long-lasting.

For many leaders, their starting point is often to ask themselves, 'What do I want my legacy to be?' At first glance you may be fooled into thinking that this is classic hubristic behaviour, but nine times out of ten at this early stage it isn't. Seeking to create a legacy is often about doing something that has a greater benefit for the whole rather than for the self.

New leader phase: be inquisitive

These early days in the role are a time when the burden of expectation is at its lowest, when the opportunity to take some (good) risks is possibly at its best, and when thinking outside the box is second-nature, as hardly any thoughts are inside this particular box at this stage. It's an interesting period of volatility, discovery and opportunity, which can either sow the seeds of a future which is balanced and inclusive, or one that is closed off and hubristic. Each move sets the tone for the ongoing trajectory.

It is an interesting period when considering the optimum stance to be taken regarding learning about a new business. Of course, it should be a period of learning and consultation by our new CEO, particularly if coming into a new sector. Leadership is a special skill, but one that is easily transferrable from one industry to another, which is why so many CEOs are appointed not just from outside a company, but also come in after having worked in a completely different sector.

It is an optimum time for leaders to be curious; in fact, curiosity should be their calling card. These early days are characterized by a desire to learn and understand, while at the same time pushing the boundaries of tried and tested ways of working. Common questions they could and should be asking are, 'why not, what if, and why?' The best leaders look beyond what is known because they realize that this is what leads to new opportunities. They are, at this stage, comfortable with not always understanding the full picture. They are not fazed by this in the slightest; indeed, it is great new leaders who embrace such a situation. They are relaxed, because they know that they are not expected to know everything.

This questioning period is, in the right hands, one characterized by a fierce commitment to learning through experimenting. They are free to have a go, to take a punt, to throw something out there, knowing that, at this stage, failure is part of the journey to long-term success.

One way of thinking about the role of CEO during the early part of this new leader phase is of it being similar to that of an external consultant. You have been brought in to look at everything from a fresh perspective but are not expected to become tied down by day-to-day operations. The focus is on ideas and strategies, not detailed implementation. The exception to this, of course, will be if the appointment of the CEO has been made at a moment of extreme crisis, in which case there would be a need to hit the ground running with practical solutions and tactics in order to avert a commercial disaster. However, in the scheme of things, that type of scenario is quite rare, so our focus here is on those new appointments that have been made during a period when there is time for this phase to be one of discovery and self-discovery.

A way for the rest of the C-suite to judge whether the choice of new CEO has been a good one is to focus, in these first few months, primarily on the level and range of inquisitiveness being demonstrated. An enquiring mind will be one that challenges every assumption, scrutinizes every existing way of doing things and suggests trying new and different approaches, however impractical they may sound.

If such a mind is working at full tilt, this period will be exhausting, stretching and even exasperating for the incumbent team. If the conversation between C-suite members and their partners every evening isn't 'Right now, we are being driven nuts by endless questions, queries and requests', then the new CEO is not being inquisitive enough. In this respect, the CEO is not conducting a charm offensive. Life should be made difficult, challenging and downright frustrating during this period.

Like an adolescent always asking, 'Why?', or a toddler's never-ending 'What's that?', our new CEO should be similarly annoying ... to good reason. Just as kids' constant questioning does end up modifying parents' outlooks and perspectives, so our CEO will shake up entrenched views and long-held assumptions whose logic and purpose have been long forgotten.

If, after a few months, those dinner-table conversations have become grudgingly modified to 'You know what, maybe some of those crazy questions weren't so mad after all', then the right effect will have been achieved. Scales will start to fall from people's eyes; some of the 'what ifs' will already have yielded some interesting results. Clear potential competitive advantages, cost-saving benefits, organizational efficiencies … whatever it is, they will have been revealed.

That is when payback and value start to accrue from this inquisitive phase. Exasperation turns into admiration, as rueful types of reactions begin to accumulate: 'Why didn't we think of that? Well, I guess that's what the CEO is paid to come up with.' This healthy state of affairs becomes the perfect platform on which to build, to move on to the next phase, horizon two, in which power can be consolidated and implementation can commence in earnest.

If, however, the CEO's inquisitive zeal becomes a series of pointless questions, some initial research and development which turn out to be blind alleys, and a growing sense of 'change for change's sake', then along the way the new CEO will have lost the hearts and minds of the team before even really getting going. If the questioning and probing just ends up seeming fanciful and irrelevant, even downright egotistical preening, then a serious issue of credibility and competence starts to emerge. If those evening conversations turn to ones of ridicule and annoyance, it can be a long, hard road back to effectiveness for our CEO, even before they get going properly.

The further danger here is what then becomes hubris alarm bell number one. The buzz of the plaudits – 'Wow, that's an interesting new angle' – becomes so addictive and beguiling that ideas and strategies are proposed based on their level of newness rather than any further considerations of the practicality or desirability of enacting them. Being thought of as an iconoclastic leader, who goes against the grain, becomes a drug, a high, regardless of the corporate carnage it leaves in its wake. As we have identified elsewhere, this becomes a delicate balancing act: choosing the path less trodden can be rewarding as long you don't end up snarled up in brambles.

New leader phase: absorb knowledge

As well as asking questions and proposing bold, original ideas, for the new CEO this should be a period of absorbing all the vital knowledge about a new sector or industry. There will be so much to learn. A classic SWOT analysis (strengths, weaknesses, opportunities and threats) could be as good a place to start as any, drawn up by the C-suite team. Internal workings, external pressures, regulatory constraints, looming pressure points in the sector, the current health of the largest competitor ... so many considerations and pressing issues.

The balancing act for an incoming leader is to take all this knowledge on board while still retaining that vital 'outsider' perspective. During the interview rounds, our new CEO will have impressed selection panels with unique insights and perspectives, challenging some or even many of the 'Well, it's always been done that way' responses from company insiders. How does our CEO keep those lightning moments and thoughts once the outsider becomes an insider?

The way to achieve this is for there to be open-mindedness on both sides. By 'sides' we mean the new CEO on one side and the incumbent board on the other. In professional football, when a new manager comes in, a completely fresh coaching team often accompanies him. In public limited companies this is rare. A key skill of the new CEO is to work with and get the best out of the (largely or completely) inherited C-suite team. This team will have been working for a previous CEO who was in phase three, that of established leader, and we will be exploring the dynamic in place there later in this chapter. The relationship with a new leader is completely different and requires some significant adjustments on both sides.

The team needs to be more open-minded and avoid falling into the trap of being overly defensive. 'This is how we've done things up to now and it has worked well' can all too easily become the stock answer to many of the new CEO's questions, regardless of whether they are naïve or sharp and incisive. Everything is in danger of being interpreted as an attack on track record and existing attitudes, when the healthier outlook is simply to realize that that was then and this is now.

Whatever strategies, decisions and tactics were played out under previous CEOs were the result of the specific combination of those CEOs' judgements in those moments in time, working with the team then. Strategies conceived and implemented at that time were the best they could have been, knowing what was then known. The double whammy of a fresh perspective and the gift of hindsight by the new CEO and the newly constituted team makes it all too easy to trash the legacy of previous managements. If the new CEO comes in with a 'let's trash the legacy' mentality, there is often the sound of hubris alarm bell number two.

It's neither big nor clever to indulge in such point scoring and, ultimately, it is somewhat pointless. It is looking backwards instead of forwards. Everyone can always learn from mistakes made, but the healthier attitude at this juncture, the moment when a new team is in place with a new leader at its head, is to think of day one as ground zero, a fresh start, a bright new day to be embraced and from which people can march forward in step.

New leader phase: be a bold challenger

If everyone can accept that attitude of 'moving forward', things are more likely to be off to a good start. The next challenge is for the new CEO to resist rapid institutionalization, becoming sucked into adopting insider status long before all the benefits of their unique outsider status have been realized. This can become a real knife-edge of hubris: all the benefits of being the outsider can also corrode into becoming arrogant behaviour. So, how to steer a correct path?

Appointing a new CEO from outside the organization comes with a considerable downside, in that there is an inevitable time lag (and we've already discussed the critical value of time) in getting up to speed on the business, its challenges, the sector, competitors, suppliers, customers ... the list goes on. The trade-off needs to be that something fresh is added: those original insights that benefit from looking at everything anew. It is then that our new CEO can be a maverick, a risk-taker, or an iconoclast. This brings excitement, energy and new ideas back into a boardroom that may well have slipped into habit and routine.

This can be a period of thrilling danger – or dreaded danger. By tearing up rulebooks and established ways of doing things, our new broom can fashion sweeping changes in a business's fortunes, just by taking a leap in the dark that no one else has dared to do or has even considered. This can either be the new leader at their thrilling best or a series of facepalm moments that soon unravel, alienating all the stakeholders we have mentioned earlier. But, hey, that risk is what was implicitly signed up to when making an external appointment.

Let's now assume that the early, daring decisions of our new leader have in fact proved to be triumphs, inspired thinking which has achieved an impressive quantum leap. Here is where hubris alarm bell number three may start to ring. The adrenalin rush of a risky decision that has paid off handsomely can become a gambler's addiction. Placing everything on red on the roulette wheel paid off the first time, so why won't it again ... and again? The plaudits for early successes, internally and from other stakeholders, plus in all likelihood the business media too, can become similarly addictive. Playing the outsider seems to be more fun than becoming an insider, so why not resist going native and becoming part of the established order? Let's keep playing the maverick, even if it is high-risk. As we have seen, Jobs, Zuckerberg, Bezos and Musk all have maverick tendencies, which for them has largely paid off. But, as we've said, the number of business leaders with the talent and genius to ride that risky trail successfully is frighteningly small.

For the more regular new CEO there comes a pivotal moment, when the outsider concedes the need to become an insider. It's when no such concession is made, when continuing to be the leader running on intuition, gut feeling and instinct presses ahead in the face of boring evidence and data to the contrary, that things can become sticky. Or when that addiction to 'originality' starts to be a problem in its own right. It's when early triumphs go to the head and begin to block the path to learning, collaboration and co-operation. Now, in their head, it is better to defy the odds, to confound the naysayers, to go against all received wisdom in order to stand out and be seen, and recognized, as a genius leader. The momentum created by early successes now helps to railroad through further, even more extreme, strategies. Argument and debate are shut down in favour of speed and decisiveness. Boldness and originality are promoted at the expense of analysis and consolidation.

Events then start to move fast. There is either a crash and burn moment, when a more extreme, hasty, gut-instinct decision goes so badly wrong that the board and shareholders *do* invoke their power to remove the nascent CEO. This, while extremely painful and even humiliating for the business is, in the wider scheme of things, a short-term blip, a sharp trauma from which matters can be recovered quickly.

The other, more difficult outcome can be where the value of the early successes is sufficiently powerful for subsequent failures, however sharp, to continue to be given the benefit of the doubt. On the back of this, a feeling of impregnability starts to set in in the mind of our CEO. The failure to take on a more inclusive, open, learning spirit is not punished and our CEO uses the early success as a base from which to ascend a continuing path of arrogance and single-mindedness. If the pivot point from outsider to insider isn't taken at the appropriate moment, then our CEO will never start to make a full, rounded contribution to the business.

Recognizing the sweet spot of that moment, when thinking outside the box has exhausted its usefulness, and the incisive use of industry/ sector knowledge is becoming more important, requires a high degree of reflection and self-knowledge. To avoid the false pride of being a permanent outsider, our CEO needs to be aware of the outsider/insider tussle and then resolve it successfully. The board needs to play an active part in this, too. They need to embrace change and fresh ideas, but have their radar tuned to the risks of change for change's sake and evidence of a CEO revelling in going out on a limb for no better reason than garnering media column inches.

Like so much in life, it's a series of tough calls, judging the right time to be bold and to take risks, and the time to take more holistic decisions. These calls are at their most acute and important in this new leader phase of a CEO.

Horizon two: the successful CEO – consolidating power

Let's now consider the next key phase in the journey of the development of a CEO. This second horizon follows a first phase of inquisitiveness and experimentation. Hopefully, the three hubris alarm bells we signposted earlier have remained silent, untriggered by excessive pride in originality for originality's sake, by point scoring against any inherited legacy, and by overconfidence sparked by some early successes. In not doing so, a balance has been struck between thinking and listening, between learning and instructing, and between confidence and humility.

Successful CEO phase: become a team-builder

All the inquisitiveness, knowledge and insights acquired, and the challenging of norms and accepted practices, will have shaken things up, disrupted the status quo and established our leader as an innovator, risk-taker and original thinker. It is now time to involve others on a more active basis, and to start sharing the load.

As we have seen above, all the questioning and disruption in the learning phase will possibly have polarized opinion. There will be those in the C-suite and beyond who initially may have felt threatened or even intimidated by this new, disruptive CEO, but on the back of some initial successes are now receptive and open to new ideas and a change of approach. There will also be those in the opposite camp, who started out determined to be open and receptive, but for whatever reason have now decided to be closed and unco-operative towards this new broom that is sweeping through the company.

Ultimately, this is all to be expected if our new leader has embraced and adopted all the phases we laid out above. To be vanilla, to generate a reaction no stronger or more opinionated than that they seem to be 'really nice', means that the CEO is unlikely to be an effective agent of change. Provoking a strong reaction is all part of what success looks like.

The challenge next, though, is to harness those strong opinions and potentially polarizing reactions into a cohesive team, one which can move the agenda along to an implementation period. Bold new ideas and interesting new strategies don't take an organization forward one single metre if they are not implemented. And a CEO cannot implement new plans alone. Effective implementation requires a team, working together with a clear common purpose and shared vision.

To create that team, which will usually be the C-suite plus potentially some key specialists and possibly some external support, too, the CEO now has some choices to make. If a consensus across the C-suite team has been cultivated from day one and is still holding firm at day one plus 100, 200 or even 500 days, then some great natural leadership skills will have enabled this. However, it is likely that among a group of senior professionals, all with, by definition, more experience in their sector than the incoming CEO, opinions – as well as assumptions and previous practices – will have been challenged.

It is at this point that a balanced approach will achieve the best results. It's time to move from being a disrupter to becoming a team-builder. The implementation of great new initiatives will only occur speedily and efficiently if every department wholeheartedly embraces it. That depends on each department head being committed to it and supporting the CEO's initiative 100 per cent. Of course, each C-suite member needs to commit to doing so; if they don't, maybe they should be considering their position. However, at this relatively early stage, the CEO can probably ill afford to lose key members of the executive team.

This brings us to yet another hubris crossroads. Expecting unquestioning commitment to a new strategy, a change of direction or a fresh vision, may, at this stage, be asking too much. The CEO needs to allow for debate, compromise and a search for consensus. To deny this may well be too much of a test of pride at this moment, a driving through of a new way of working which is not yet fully proven. The hubristic leader, at this juncture, will push through a plan with no thought for the cohesiveness of the team. They will be too afraid that any suggestion of compromise will be interpreted as weakness and indecision to allow any deviation from a declared plan. What is won in terms of clarity and decisiveness can be lost in a failure to bring hearts and minds along on the journey.

This is, of course, the central quandary of leadership. Lead at all costs or seek consensus: which is it to be? At this stage of the CEO's journey, provided that a bedrock of respect has been established through a mix of bold ideas, early successes and astute listening, then at this specific point some concessions can afford to be made, in the interests of creating a team which is pulling in the same direction. Develop some consolidation of achievement through consensus and there will be more appropriate moments in the future, during the third phase, when things can be moved on again.

If this all sounds rather Machiavellian, a little too much of 'keep your friends close and your enemies closer', it need not, and should not, be that cold and calculating. Rather, you are working to develop a team that becomes greater than the sum of its parts. By working together in pursuit of a clear, distinctive CEO driven vision, everybody wins. For a great leader, there is greater satisfaction in a shared rather than a solitary triumph. To have been seen to engineer a success which was co-ordinated smoothly across all disciplines within the business, and which was therefore implemented at optimum speed and efficiency, reflects more fulsomely on the CEO. Not only has a bold initiative been conceived, it has also been carried out with maximum efficiency as a result of a rounded set of skills: project co-ordination, planning and, yes, team-building.

Successful CEO phase: become an enabler

To sustain this success as a team-builder, the CEO needs to throw another element into the mix, that of then enabling the team members to develop their skills, confidence and decision-making abilities. Having led by example in perhaps the implementation of a first full-blown initiative, the time has come to hand over the reins, entirely or in part, to the rest of the C-suite team.

This is where hubris once again has the potential to rear its head. Flush with the success of project implementation and of having a team operating either fully in harmony, or at least giving the impression of harmony to the outside world, does our CEO choose to keep control or relinquish some of it?

In a large, complex organization, control freakery will always end up being a limiting factor. Holding on to power invariably results in diminishing returns, but enabling others to take decisions, to come up with innovative ideas that have some prospect of being listened to and developed, takes both confidence and humility. To wrest from yourself the glory of exclusively setting the agenda for the goals, vision and strategy for the business can be hard. But by prompting and enabling others to think in new ways, to come up with solutions and in turn to enable their teams, you now have the whole company pushing in the same direction, instead of it being driven only from the top.

It's about being generous, enabling people to develop their true potential, of not being afraid of others having ideas, and the opportunity to build on and develop your original concept. This is the point where the CEO becomes a mentor to their team, passing on skills and ways of thinking that empower the whole team to learn and develop. Ideally, this establishes a particular momentum running through the company, with the mentored C-suite appreciating the benefits of this process and working it down through their reporting line, and so on.

If the setting of this example of mentoring and enabling starts at the very top, with the CEO, it will have the best chance of being a process that continues to flow right through the organization. However, if it isn't seen to emanate from the top, the impulse to share learning immediately has far less impetus.

So, this hubristic crossroads – whether or not to share knowledge (and possible glory) with others – has wide-ranging implications for the business. It either opens up a democratizing process of sharing knowledge (and knowledge is power) or it doesn't. The choice is in the CEO's hands.

Successful CEO phase: become a collaborator

Feeding off this impulse to enable others and to share knowledge is a wider spirit of collaboration. As well as passing skills, knowledge and ways of thinking down, this is the impulse to work alongside others. Those who are chosen to work alongside can be the widest possible set of people and organizations. It can be internal as well as external collaboration of all types, with the CEO the best-placed person to open various doors that might otherwise be closed to certain people within the business.

The internal collaboration aspect is all about setting an example for others to follow. As with enabling, it is about leading the way in drawing together potentially conflicting elements in order to find solutions. A typical example of this might be setting up and chairing a project management group, and very pointedly including the HR director where there has been evidence of other departments failing to consult in that area.

However, the most interesting part of the collaboration process for a CEO is externally. Is your business seen to be an industry leader, or a significant opinion-former in your sector? Or is it considered secretive and inscrutable, deliberately closed off to the world? In this age of social media, there is no question about which approach the most important judges of a business – its customers – prefer. Businesses that are seen as open, transparent, sharing and participatory (in the widest sense) are the ones to which consumers and the media will warm. Such transparency can, of course, quite legitimately have its limits, as, in the end, competitive advantage still needs to be sought by all appropriate means. But a CEO who has, and is seen to have, a wider, inclusive agenda is one who will end up with greater respect and wider influence.

Gaining influence with industry bodies and regulators, with suppliers and competitors, and even with government only comes by reaching out and participating. Any external body will sit up and take notice of the personal involvement of a CEO in a way that no other job title in the business can achieve. On that basis, a CEO must use the unique power of their position and title in imaginative and constructive ways. Forging stronger links with the local community, with chosen charities, with trade associations, and with key suppliers – all have a payback which is part of that development of a broader vision and purpose for the business. The CEO sets the tone and creates the agenda.

It is here that the context of a situation is so important. Have you ever had this reaction to a media moment? The latest results of a major business are being discussed on air, for example on BBC Radio 4's *Today* programme, or a Sky News TV business slot, and put up for the interview is the finance director, not the CEO. You spend the next three minutes not listening properly to the interview, so distracted are you by the fact that it is not the CEO being interrogated. Why is it the finance director speaking? Does this mean there is a focus on some financial irregularity? Has the CEO been struck down with a serious illness? Does the business have something to hide? With all those theories swirling around in your head, you completely miss that in fact it was a positive set of results.

All this reaching out with invitations to collaborate and co-operate is a sign of strength, not weakness. However, you often see, in proud, hubristic CEOs, an interpretation that is quite the reverse. Trade associations are seen as 'talking shops' and 'old boy networks'. Suppliers are to be kept at arm's length to keep them hungry and to ensure that negotiations remain hard-nosed. Reaching out to talk to the local community and directly to customers will mean exposing yourself to endless spurious complaints and single-issue arguments. Better to hunker down and get on with the real business of focusing on competitive advantage. Collaboration is for wimps.

In the twentieth century you could just about get away with such a combative, isolationist stance. These days, not so much. The court of public opinion has a wider set of judgements against organizations now. Accountability for ethical and environmental considerations has never been higher. As the public face of the business, the modern CEO has to face the music. The canny, thoughtful ones are tackling this proactively, setting the agenda rather than responding to it, leading the debate as opposed to being dragged into it. By agreeing to be accessible and open to being challenged and argued with, the good CEO can become great; and by great we mean by taking their profile, and that of the business, to the next level. By being an opinion-former, the CEO and the company are stronger and more able to face and react to an increasingly complex set of measurements against which performance is assessed.

Successful CEO phase: become an implementer

Finally, in relation to this 'horizon two' phase of a CEO's tenure, there now needs to be some action. Learning, consulting and collaborating, and enabling and building a cohesive team is all well and good, but ultimately will mean little if it is not translated into meaningful activity. It's time to get things done; the markets now need to start seeing results. The CEO and the assembled team need to be able to be judged against tangible shifts in performance.

The skill here is for the CEO to decide on the optimum time to enact a new strategy. In Chapter 6 we talked about the balance between collaboration and urgency, and this is the key moment in the CEO's journey when this needs to be resolved. This is the time for collaboration and enabling to bear fruit and be turned into something which can be enacted and then measured. For as William Goldman said, 'No one knows anything' and this can still be true of any new strategy. Until it is launched to customers, you never fully know if something is going to be a success. And customers are fickle and capricious, with always a part of them that is unfathomable, no matter how exhaustive the research.

This new strategy, product, market opportunity, whatever it may be, has the CEO's name on it. There is now no hiding place. If it's a success, the balanced CEO will make a point of sharing the spoils and the glory with all relevant participants, which effectively means the whole company. By all means don't be shy in coming forward to publicize success, but almost immediately show that a hunger for it is just a step in a process, a reason to carry on delivering, and learning from it in order to inform the next initiative. The skill lies not in downplaying success, but neither to milk it; complacency is an obvious by-product of success. It is the CEO who should be leading the way in fighting any whiff of complacency by pushing the team immediately on to the next project.

The proud, hubristic leader seeks to claim all the credit and to be the centre of attention, thus, at the moment of triumph, dissipating many of the morale-boosting and team-building consequences of success. Be generous in victory (and, just as importantly, in defeat), otherwise, ironically, winning can leave a bitter taste.

Horizon three: the danger zone. The confident, established leader

We come to the third and final act in our CEO drama. It's one that's already had a bit of everything – intrigue, tension, suspense, action. Now comes the denouement, and it is one which can settle into complacency, leaving the audience underwhelmed and disappointed.

Established leader phase: keep reinventing

The skill now is to remain as inquisitive and creative as in horizon one, as if horizon two had not been initiated. Our CEO is now fully an insider; it is inevitable and not necessarily all bad. Insider knowledge leads to a faster, more in-depth understanding of the original SWOT analysis and of industry/sector issues. The C-suite team is now your team, not an inherited one. The successes to build on are yours, as are the mistakes to be learned from. This is all positive.

However, to keep pushing yourself back into horizon one mode, one of restlessly challenging everything, is now much harder, because effectively you are questioning and challenging your own track record and legacy. It may have been easy enough to create some quick wins and a couple of blinding new insights when coming in from the outside, but now it's difficult and complicated. It requires focus, hunger and drive. If the material benefits have been bestowed on the CEO in the form of well-earned profit-related bonuses and options, then all too soon the only driving forward that is being done on a regular basis is on the golf course.

Now, the hunger becomes driven less by success and more by the prospect of carving out a legacy. There should already be a desire to think ahead, long term, about the values and purpose that will be left behind once you are no longer sitting at the head of the boardroom table. This in itself should provide sufficient incentive and impetus not to rest on your laurels but instead to seek out the broader, deeper impact of your tenure.

Established leader phase: keep being challenged

Part of the reinvention process also involves ensuring that you are surrounded by people who will keep you on your toes. The danger in this third phase is that the CEO will have gradually (or maybe even suddenly) surrounded themselves with a team of their choosing which is less challenging than the team which was inherited upon arrival. If asked to jump and the response is just 'how high?', that sort of team will no longer be an adequate sounding board for bringing out the best in the CEO. Instead of being *complementary*, it is merely *complimentary*. By now, of course, the board should be pulling in the same direction, but while still being capable of challenging and stretching the CEO.

The self-aware and balanced CEO recognizes this and even consciously retains, or employs, those spiky individuals who always provide an interesting and provocative alternative viewpoint. It is the lazy, hubristic leader who is surrounded by people who just say 'yes', individuals who are ultimately as lazy as the leader in that regard.

The selection of cabinet ministers has been shown to follow a similar trend. Individuals are selected based on their relationship with the incoming leader, their demonstrated loyalty and similar views. Yet diversity of thought is a much needed capability, which can be found lacking. The code of collective responsibility, of all being accountable for the policy decisions, is a great way to ensure party discipline and in fact is an equally good model for a C-suite to adopt. A united, coherent message is vital in setting out a clear purpose and strategy and in laying out a solid set of values to abide by. However, to arrive at that consensus there must still be vigorous debate behind closed doors. Great leaders encourage this; tyrants, bullies and dictators suppress it. History has never been on the side of the latter, and any CEO looking to build a lasting legacy needs to be mindful of this in the level of debate and discussion that they may choose to encourage.

Negotiating the three horizons

Through each stage we have seen that there are choices to be made, moments when a CEO can either turn in a humble, inclusive, learning, legacy-creating direction, or fall into the temptation of grabbing short-term glory, focused on self-interest and usually at the expense of others. In the final chapters we will lay out the 10 key lessons that need to be carried forward in order to slay the hubris dragon permanently.

CHAPTER 8

A Better Way to Lead

We have laid bare a fair number of examples of hubristic behaviour in well-known business leaders, showing how easy it can be to stray into adopting proud and ultimately destructive leadership traits. Many of these leaders are people whom others seek to emulate, seeing their high-stakes, buccaneering exploits as having more upsides than down, despite the obvious risks. But it is the extremely rare spark of genius possessed by a Steve Jobs or a Jeff Bezos that just about navigates them through to triumph. The 1 per cent rarity of that spark does not mean that these leaders are not at risk of crashing and burning – far from it. It just means they may stay at the helm for slightly longer than the other 99 per cent.

Successful, sustained leadership requires constant reappraisal and self-reflection. In essence, leaders need to develop and operate according to a set of checks and balances to ensure that their stewardship of the business remains positive, outward-looking and purposeful.

There are seven key **Leadership Reflections**, which, if adopted and followed, can lead to sustainable business success:

1. Know and define your values and your purpose.
2. Cultivate connections.
3. Value diversity.
4. Be truly coachable.
5. Dismantle hierarchies.
6. Nurture aspiration.
7. Embrace self-reflection.

Let's explore each of these in more detail.

1. Know and define your values and your purpose

As we have already discussed, it is now vital, more than ever before, that every business sets out a distinctive set of values and a purpose for its business. Stakeholders typically demand not only a clear ethical and environmental stance from an organization, but also want to understand better the larger role that companies fulfil in relation to wider societal issues, using this information as a key part of forming their judgement and opinion about the company.

Increasingly, employees, particularly millennials and Gen Z, will decide their career path based as much on the values and purpose of that business as on the remuneration package. Likewise, in the battle for the hearts of consumers, it is those businesses that are most closely aligned to their values that will win their long-term loyalty. It is therefore more important that the CEO is clear on what their business stands for and that this is actively used as part of their leadership compass.

How to focus on values

The media, analysts, social media commentators, satirical talk shows and all kinds of outlets are calling out authenticity failings and hypocrisy. Greenwash, false claims about gender or pay ratio equality, tax haven activity, there is a growing list of topics on which CEOs and their organizations are being called out. At the time of writing, we find ourselves in the middle of the global coronavirus pandemic. Businesses across the world are, directly or indirectly, drawing on government aid in unprecedented fashion. There have been embarrassing U-turns by some organizations who have claimed, for example, furlough subsidies when they are run by well-heeled celebs or are exposed as paying no tax in that domicile. People do not forget hypocrisy like this, and the reputational damage to a company may well prove to be long-lasting.

Authenticity breeds trust and trust is the most valuable but the hardest won asset a business can have. The word 'trust' is often bandied about without an appreciation for how critical it is for organizational success. Leaders who can convey with conviction what matters to them and why, and how it links to a broader and higher purpose, will inspire and connect people. A committed employee will always go the extra mile; will spread word of the business to everyone around them; and will display unwavering loyalty. Loyalty is as hard won as trust, but in a world when every employee is just a LinkedIn click away from a new career opportunity, it is another huge asset.

If the argument that a strong set of values is important, how should a leader set about defining them and adhering to them?

The starting point for a CEO is to find your true north; in knowing what you value and what matters to you, the goal is then to align your values to the organization's purpose.

While we may not engage in many conversations about personal values, the truth is that they are embedded in who we are, the way we act and in our modes of behaviour. How we behave is how our values manifest themselves to others. When a wide range of stakeholders (employees, shareholders, investors, suppliers and customers) are studying our behaviour as a reflection of our values, having a thought-through set of values is vital.

What purpose do personal values serve?

- knowing what your values and your core principles are enables you to apply them consistently;
- awareness of what is important to you – what motivates you, or your reasons for becoming and staying a leader – enables alignment of personal values with company values and purpose;
- core values can be used to guide your decisions;
- values are the litmus test for the choices we make;
- people respect and value leaders who are honest;
- our personal values inform the things that we choose to do or not to do;
- values act as a compass to help guide you to make better decisions and help you to articulate the things that are important to you;
- values serve as the foundation for your purpose, for what you truly seek in life and they help build your personal capacity;

- by bringing to the surface the things that are most likely to engage us, interest us and align most closely with the things that we feel passionate about – and which, at the end of the day, matter to us – we can start to frame what our purpose is.

A successful business in the 2020s must have a clear purpose and a set of values that can be endorsed and embraced by its employees and, most importantly, by its customers. At this point, we'd like to throw out a challenge to get you, the reader, to take a few moments to reflect on your own values and purpose, in order for these to become the foundation for the values and purpose of the business you are running.

Define your values and purpose

Take some time to reflect on your values; below you will see some questions that can help you to frame them. Write them down and try to formulate your dream goal, end goal, performance goal and process goals. In this way, values become grounded in the nitty gritty of business activity. Values need to be linked to goals, to process, to tactics as well as strategy.

An interesting exercise to conduct is to think about and document a number of different iterations of a set of values in order to crystallize and test them to ensure that you have been honest and that they represent *you* (and not merely what you think people are expecting to see). This can be tough, as it may mean discarding some values that you know to be popular, to have virtue and to be ones which are attractive to customers and to employees.

At the time of writing, the world is still coming to terms with the coronavirus pandemic, both in the short term, in how to understand the devastation it has inflicted on the global economy, and in the longer term, the wider re-evaluation it has prompted on issues such as inequality and the environment. Now, more than ever, is a time to reappraise and define a set of values and a purpose fit for a post-pandemic world.

The environment is changing

Firstly, let's focus on attitudes towards the environment. The pandemic forced a drastic short-term change in international movements and attitudes to travel more generally. It showed that huge changes to the way we think about the natural world and our place in it can occur if something forces us all to adapt and change. At the same time, a tiny unseen virus is proving to be a health enigma in terms of easy routes to a vaccine, and has brought humanity around the world to its knees. It is a sharp reminder that humans do not hold sway over nature but are just one part of a complex, interrelated, interdependent ecosystem.

In this changed climate and culture, environmental concerns have been thrown into sharp focus. So, right now, are you *really* concerned about the environment or do you just pay lip service to it? Does your personal lifestyle display any signs of modification in the most recent five years, over which period it could be said that climate change and carbon emissions have become an unavoidable fact? Are you flying less? What type of car do you drive? Petrol, diesel or electric?

The global restrictions on flying caused by the pandemic have led to a major reappraisal of what constitutes essential business travel, with Zoom conferences replacing, possibly permanently, global get-togethers. Notwithstanding that imposed change, was such a modification of behaviour even remotely on your radar before the arrival of Covid-19? Does your household own a gas-guzzling 4x4, for you to drive to the office in order to chair a meeting about green initiatives for the business? Is that even a disjunction that you would recognize or concede? If those green initiatives incurred a significant material cost to the business, with only a slim prospect of long-term payback, how much importance would you ascribe to them?

The environment as an issue is one where walking the walk as well as talking the talk can be critical. The media, employees and customers are growing impatient with green hypocrisy and if there is a yawning gap between your pronouncements and your deeds, and even in your lifestyle, then you may well be held to account in the court of public opinion.

It was widely reported that the World Economic Forum (WEF) meeting at Davos in January 2019, which hosted a series of talks on the dangers of man-made climate change, was attended by a set of delegates who arrived via the largest number of private jet flights, some 1,500, of any WEF meeting. All the worthy 'initiatives' and 'communiqués' that emanated from that summit were overshadowed and undercut by this glaring hypocrisy. Whatever the practicalities that private jets afford (security, speed, flexibility), this was as big a private jet own goal as those cap-in-hand flights taken by motor industry moguls to Washington when seeking that bailout we mentioned in Chapter 3.

Black Lives Matter

Another notable shift that has occurred is the emergence of the #BlackLivesMatter (BLM) debate as a key issue, galvanized by the tragic death of George Floyd in May 2020 at the hands of the Minneapolis police. While centred on the US, the issues this has raised have reverberated around the world. Knowledge of black history; the judgement of history of the slave trade; the social and health inequalities of black people thrown into sharp focus by the coronavirus pandemic; these are all overdue debates now being conducted. And the attitudes and track records of the corporate world in relation to BAME (Black, Asian and Minority Ethnic) people are also being scrutinized. Just as the gender pay gap remains an area where corporations are still playing catch-up, so the representation of BAME people on boards and the implementation of robust and consistent anti-racist policies are areas where, in general, the track record is at best patchy and more often woeful.

The strength of feeling stimulated by BLM issues across a wide consensus of society, among white people as well as BAME, highlights that this is not a fringe concern that can be consigned to being fixed by indulging in some superficial, cosmetic, box-ticking measures. It requires a significant attitudinal shift towards a more active promotion of equality of opportunity. As a wake-up call, BLM issues need to be heeded, acted upon and included as an important part of the values and purpose of a business.

What is the level of ethnic minority representation in your C-suite? In the UK, a government-backed initiative has created a 'One by 2021' target for all FTSE 100 companies. By December 2020, with less than a year to go, 37 per cent of these companies still had no 'One' in place. Across Western economies, this is a systemic issue, and one that may be hard to fix in a generation, let alone in one year. But just as thousands of companies are playing a desperate game of catch-up in relation to fixing the gender pay gap as a result of decades of inaction, so it is with opportunities for BAME people. If you never start, you never get there. Now is the time to start, with the BLM movement providing a timely impetus for us all.

Just these couple of issues, of green attitudes and BAME representation on boards, show that tackling and fixing things may prove to be an uncomfortable process. Looking yourself in the eye and testing whether not only the values and beliefs you say you hold are ones that you honestly believe, but also that you're prepared to take demonstrable action to fix things, can be a sobering truth game.

Having regrets about inaction and a lack of priority to such issues in the past is a waste of time and energy; we are where we are. The important thing now is to re-evaluate priorities and to act. The most important reaction to the fact that BLM has brought the corrosive effect of attitudes towards ethnic minorities to the fore is not to worry about why this had not been higher up the corporate agenda up until now. The important thing is to have the humility to take the message on board and to act upon it as most appropriate within your business.

Questions to help to define your personal values

As part of the exercise of looking at yourself in the mirror and scrutinizing your authenticity, ask yourself these questions and write down your answers:

- What are my life's goals and ambitions?
- Honestly, what are the values that are most important to me personally? Why are they important?
- How do I bring these values to life? In what ways do they show up?
- What are my strengths – the talents I personally bring to the table?
- What are the values I want my business to be identified with?
- At the end of the day, what do I want to have accomplished and be known for; what will my legacy be?
- What am I most passionate about; how is this demonstrated at work?
- Do my values and the values of the business align?
- Do these values reflect who I am in every aspect of my life, i.e. both at work and at home?
- What values would people say I exhibit on a regular basis?

The values you write down should serve to anchor and frame the way you hold yourself to account. Take some time to review the values you have chosen – do they truly represent you? Do they reflect the actions you take and the way you behave? In the cold light of day, do they reflect what you really stand for?

Applying your values at work

Your statement of values and goals should then become a living document that you return to regularly. You can then reflect on whether you are behaving in a way that is honouring those values and progressing towards achieving the goals. If not, what has led you off track and how can you get back on the right track?

A strong focus on values and goals that have been declared publicly means that it can be more easily recognized when a CEO starts to deviate from this and displays signs of behaving in more self serving, hubristic ways. The balanced CEO will have set up two aligned methods of judgement on their performance: their own benchmarking against the written-down values, while at the same time welcoming the judgement of peers and other stakeholders.

This same process then cascades downwards. A good leader, developing others, will encourage them to explore *their* values and translate these into goals in the same way. Part of the role of an effective CEO is to ensure that there is a consistent purpose to this chain of values as it is framed, and then working to implement it throughout the organization.

The challenge for leaders is, surprisingly, not in defining their core principles and values but in staying true to them over time and ensuring that they remain the constant that guards against temptations that may come with power and the heady heights of success. Staying true to them is another benchmark of authenticity and of openness and honesty. That consistency over time cannot be sustained if the whole thing is an act, or one is just going through the motions of being seen to be a principled and values-driven leader. At some point, sooner or later, the mask will slip, and any self-serving agenda will be exposed. And if anything provokes universal scorn, it is not just being self-serving, it is being a self-serving *hypocrite*. As we have said, authenticity ultimately cannot be faked, as, of course, it is then no longer authentic. Which brings us to the next point...

Be authentic
In every walk of life, the quality which is increasingly valued above most others is authenticity. 'Be yourself' is not just a glib motivational poster headline; it is a vitally important instruction. Politicians, entertainers, sports stars ... you name it, the people we look up to and admire are those who appear to be relatable, honest, down-to-earth and, yes, authentic. We say 'appear to be' and that, of course, is the great debate. In public and corporate life, ultimately one can never

tell who is being completely 'real'. However, we need to commit to an act of faith that what we see is what we get. If we take a cynical view that the whole world is an elaborate hall of mirrors, where nothing can be trusted to be what it seems to be, the authenticity debate can never be resolved.

However, what is usually true is that, over time, if you are not authentic you will be found out. The strain of maintaining the elaborate charade of appearing to be one thing when really you are something else eventually causes something to snap. People have a sixth sense for authenticity. You may not be able to prove it, but you can somehow smell and taste it. The leader whose authenticity is cast into doubt has their authority fatally undermined.

One of the most admired and popular politicians in the world today is New Zealand's Jacinda Ardern. She took office in 2017 aged 37 and her approval ratings have remained sky-high, even in the middle of the coronavirus pandemic, a situation which proved to be a tough crisis for all world leaders to handle correctly. 'Open, honest and effective' seems to be the epithet most used to describe her leadership, a decent summary of the qualities needed to be an authentic leader.

It can be argued that this is where twenty-first-century business leadership is put most sharply to the test. In simpler times, all of say, 20–30 years ago, a CEO could be judged a great leader if the simple benchmarks of profitability and shareholder value were achieved year after year. The values and purpose required to satisfy those needs were a belief in capitalism and … that's about it. How that was achieved, provided it was lawful, was open season, with wealth generation seen as a sufficient virtue to cover the values and purpose part of the annual report.

Now, more than ever as we enter the third decade of the century, such a scenario is simply not good enough. It's not sufficient for the long-term success of the business and it's not a broad enough range of values to create a meaningful legacy for any self-respecting CEO. The good news is that this spotlight on authenticity and on values and purpose shines a bright light into corners where hubris can lurk. By demanding that the business be open, honest, authentic and that it adheres to a range of ethical standards, the CEO cannot fail to be the same. It becomes a virtuous circle. Openness, honesty and a clear, ethically sound set of values in the CEO will, or should, translate into those same qualities being displayed by the business. If, as Jacinda Ardern's popularity ratings would seem to indicate, those are all attributes that lead to admiration and success, then as the business succeeds more strongly by adopting them, so the CEO can double down on pursuing that course ... and so on.

What authenticity looks like

Part of walking the walk is proving by your deeds that you believe in the values you put forward.

- you constantly seek to identify tangible examples of how you apply your values in your everyday life;
- the actions and decisions you make are congruent with your values and principles;
- your values are demonstrably reflected in what you do and say – you are authentic in how you talk about them and you can paint a picture of what that looks like in a way that resonates with stakeholders;
- people are clear about what you stand for because they see consistency, honesty and transparency;
- you paint a vivid, aspirational picture of what can be achieved, and you engage and motivate people, inspiring commitment and results – but you also keep things honest and authentic, bringing people with you on a journey where everyday successes matter, too; and
- you are not afraid to acknowledge when you get things wrong.

Authenticity self-assessment

We spend a lot of time focused on honing our core leadership capabilities, but often neglect to delve into what authenticity actually looks like. Largely this is because most of us believe, or at least want to believe, that our authenticity is without question and therefore does not require validation. The truth, however, is that authenticity in its truest sense is not as cut and dried as we may imagine.

Let's delve into that. Below are a series of questions that represent ways in which authentic behaviours are displayed. Take the time to study the questions and answer them honestly. Answering these questions in that way will be a great first step. However, the best way to validate these, if you feel ready, is to compare your perceived view of yourself with how others see you. To achieve this, ask your team to anonymously answer the same set of questions about you, and then compare the results. If there are significant disparities in the answers, this can be tough to face up to, but as an exercise in benchmarking it can be crucial.

- how often do you seek out the ideas and opinions of others?
- when you seek input or advice, how frequently do you restrict input to being from the same group of people?
- conversely, how frequently do you reach out to new and diverse sources of input and advice?
- how frequently do you engage in the practice of asking people questions with the specific intention of learning from them?
- do you actively ask people to challenge you and your decisions?
- when you encounter a high level of opposition or resistance to a course of action you have proposed and feel strongly about, what is your typical response?
- when you make the wrong decision, or make a mistake, how likely are you to share this with others?
- can you list your top three strengths?
- are you clear about what your three top areas for improvement are? If so, please list them;
- why do you see these as being areas for improvement?
- on balance, what percentage of your time do you spend on your own personal development? This should be seen as time spent improving the areas that you see as most important to your role as a leader;

- is it common for you to spend time connecting your decisions and actions back to the values and purpose of your company?
- do you believe that people describe you as someone whom they deem to be consistent, i.e. are your behaviour and actions consistent with your beliefs and values?

By having a strong sense of your personal purpose and values, and by answering these searching questions honestly, you are in a position to solidify them into a cohesive, consistent and authentic set of beliefs and values. The next step is to translate how these elements fit in and align with the purpose and values for the business.

As we have stated, the narrow, prosaic purpose of making a profit and enhancing shareholder value is, in the context of the 2020s, just that – narrow and prosaic. It's a building block for sure, as without it you cannot hope to increase the prosperity of all relevant stakeholders. However, just as the range of expected values has widened, so have the requirements of a business's purpose become more elevated. Both trends serve as a buffer against hubris. When the principal business impulses, and the only key ones being judged against, are an increase in power and profit, then that's a perfect recipe for the encouragement of greed, selfishness, pride … and hubris.

When purpose needs to be higher than that – one which is in tune with a more caring, sharing, fair and inclusive business outlook – then the instincts and behaviour associated with hubris stand out against and jar with everything else the business does and stands for. Look for this, though: there is an insidious hubris-driven higher purpose that is really a lower purpose and that is virtue-signalling.

Virtue-signalling – more hypocrisy

The term 'virtue-signalling' was apparently coined as recently as 2015 and is a classic by-product of social media interaction. It is a great, pithy term, something we have seen all too often on social media, along with that other disingenuous device, the humblebrag. Both are contemptible and laughable, the last two things a CEO and a business should be seen as being. While the humblebrag is usually no more than a demonstration of personal weakness and vanity posted on Facebook or Twitter, virtue-signalling comes from a similar wellspring of poor judgement but can fatally undermine the credibility of a business's shot at a higher purpose. Just as employees and customers have finely tuned noses to sniff out a lack of authenticity, when reaching for a higher purpose topples over into posturing and preaching, then the audience soon sees what the overenthusiastic PR team failed to notice.

The whole thing is a minefield, with so many opportunities to get it wrong or to display a tone-deaf approach. Here are just some examples:

- Having operated for decades in a sector that has a poor record on a specific ethical issue, to suddenly pronounce that you condemn it and plan to fix it. You need to have some sort of track record of activism prior to this convenient about-turn.
- Choosing to jump on the bandwagon of a current issue, event or charitable cause with which your business has no inherent link, as a blatant piece of opportunism.
- Espousing an ideal or a cause in such a way that it is intended to portray non-participants, i.e. people not choosing to buy your product or service, as somehow failing that cause.
- Spurious or misleading charity donation angles to involvement with your company and its products.

There are many more ways, too, in which businesses have found to virtue-signal their shiny new higher purpose and most of them are just another huckster approach to winning business. The fact that they are dressed up as supposedly being the opposite of that makes them a savage blow to authenticity. To avoid all this is simple: be virtuous by acting virtuously and then let others judge those actions. Just as virtue-signalling scorn goes viral, so too do 'above and beyond' ways of conducting your business. They may take longer, but you are in this for the long term, aren't you?

From values to defining a higher purpose at work

That diversion was for a purpose, not a higher one, but a practical one. Have the nagging question, 'is this just virtue-signalling?' in the back of your mind when formulating your higher purpose, and you will avoid its pitfalls.

Our higher purpose doesn't need to be, and in fact shouldn't be, some sanctimonious twaddle that is designed to look good rather than do good. It must spring genuinely and truthfully from the CEO's values, and from the shared values agreed by the business. Let's also be clear: if that higher purpose *does* end up creating greater loyalty from the range of stakeholders, then don't feel guilty about that. This is a happy by-product that may well result in greater profitability. That profitability doesn't sully or demean the purpose as long as it is one that has been pursued, to use that word again, authentically.

Higher purpose urges leaders to think and aim higher, and beyond mere profit. It enables leaders to connect profit with purpose, integrating this combination into an organization's framework as a fundamental component for the workforce of today and tomorrow. Purpose can be the glue that defines an organization's identity and frames the societal need that it meets.

When looking at your own organization, here are some key elements that must be embodied within its purpose:

1. Passion: is your purpose inspiring and does it ignite passion? Do you have a clear view of why your organization exists? What problem is it helping to solve in society at large? How does it answer a real need in society? Is it likely to be as pertinent tomorrow as it is today? If not, why not? Does it reflect your organization's resilience during uncertain times?

2. Presence: is your purpose compelling, clear and apparent to both customers and stakeholders? Have they been given sufficient information to identify and enunciate it over and above simply what the organization creates or markets?

3. Alignment: does your purpose mirror your organization's roots and history? Does it motivate the C-suite team and beyond to take action?

4. Integration: are the organization's commitments harmonious with its purpose? Does the company walk its talk and carry out that purpose with passion and conviction?

5. Advocacy: does your purpose generate higher levels of loyalty in customers and stakeholders? Would they endorse the organization to others based upon its purpose?

The key question to be answered is 'what societal need(s) do we fill?' Purpose reframes your organization's contract with the world. It views social responsibility as an opportunity rather than an obligation. Those in a purpose-based organization believe that if it vanished tomorrow, the world would have lost something of great value. Purpose has an aspirational slant that creates a vision of what the organization can become. This extends above and beyond brand positioning and this year's set of results. In a purpose-based organization, values, culture and ethos are all aligned.

We started this section with values and purpose as the first point, as these are the foundation for everything that follows in points 2–7. Without this solid base, these other aspects cannot happen and, without them in place, the key defences against hubris are missing – they are *that* fundamental.

2. Cultivate connections

Another important way to ensure that, as a CEO, you stay grounded is to interact with as wide a circle of people as possible. We've suggested that the boardroom has the potential to be an ivory tower, but there is immense value in 'managing by walking about'. Making time to get up and out of your office means that your views and opinions are less likely to become fixed or narrow.

There is another benefit, however, and that is the important one of being seen to be reaching out and embracing the opinions of others. Are comments such as 'oh, we no longer see the CEO about the place', 'I've never seen the CEO in person' or 'the CEO has no idea what we do' the sorts of views that you would like to be associated with? Of course not. Don't isolate yourself. Don't limit the people you interact with every day. Seek out the opinions of others when making decisions. Have lunch, meet, travel, engage regularly with peers, and just wander about the organization. If this last one sounds a bit aimless, it is anything but. It is the serendipity of random encounters throughout the length and breadth of your business that can yield some of the most surprising yet valuable insights. Socialize and meet with people who *don't* think in the same way as you, who share different or even opposing views. This ensures that you avoid simply receiving the same feedback and unwavering support, which can make it easier for you to start believing that you know everything.

Making time for all this and sustaining a high level of variety to your interactions cannot be achieved simply through some vague commitment to 'get out of the office a bit more'. You need to develop and cultivate an entire ecosystem to ensure that you stay curious about learning. It means finding ways to look at things from an outside-in perspective. This is the viewpoint that we saw in Chapter 7 as being so precious and valuable in horizon one – the learning phase for a new leader. By cultivating a diverse and honest learning ecosystem, you can put off the day, possibly forever, of being so absorbed in the established culture of a business that the precious outsider perspective has all but disappeared.

So who should be in this learning ecosystem? Broadly, there are four types of connections that should be built up and sustained:

1. Your buffer connections: these are the ones that serve to counterbalance your constraining beliefs. Through encouragement and support these will be the people you seek out when you are

looking for emotional support. They are empathetic, good at listening and are there to do just that – listen. These are probably your closest, warmest, most personal connections with whom you can share your most unguarded thoughts. These therefore require a high level of trust and honesty, on both sides, in order to be sustained and developed. These may well be drawn from friends and family, probably from long before you took up your current post. This group can also include trusted mentors with whom you have worked through the years.

These connections are particularly valuable in helping to sustain that outside-in perspective, as they will be drawn from people who are currently outsiders to the organization you are running. How much you choose to burden them with questions and opinions related to any level of detail about the work issues facing you is always down to personal choice. You do not want to sour or prejudice a valuable personal friendship by quizzing them on issues of no interest or relevance to them, where the unstated response is probably: 'Why are you asking me about this?' A relationship built on trading banter can quickly lose all its spark and fun if it suddenly starts to resemble a boardroom briefing.

However, if a successful blurring of work and life boundaries can be achieved, where your personal, external connections can enrich your thinking and your perspective, then be active in cultivating this and look on it as a key part of your learning ecosystem.

2. Your expansive connections: these connections help to expand and stretch you. Define these as individuals who bring something that you do not possess, but which you are keen to learn about or gain insight into. They will challenge you to see things differently. They are another outsider view but this time they are exclusively work-related relationships. These are people who come from different backgrounds and sectors and will therefore be able to provide a fresh perspective on issues.

Seek out connections in the public sector, in academia, in government, in medicine, in the charity sector; people whose primary focus is removed from that of purely making a profit. In helping to shape and focus your thinking on the values and purpose of your organization, these sorts of people, as opposed to other profit-driven CEOs, will provide you with ideas and perspectives that can be both valuable and challenging.

Closer to home, or, should we say, to business, there are so many avenues and opportunities for seeking out and cultivating expansive connections. Think of them as outward-spreading concentric circles of possible connections:

- the circles start right here in the boardroom, with your direct C-suite reporting line. Are you maximizing the input of each member or just focusing on any natural areas of bias? For example, if your background is sales and marketing, is the head of that department the one you turn to first and therefore neglect the input of HR or finance?
- a next circle could be who *they* know and turn to. Without unduly muscling in on relationships which C-suite members may have with others, ask the question of what independent thinkers they would be happy to recommend and to welcome you talking to;
- out from that is the networking infrastructure associated with your industry or sector. Your suppliers; your trade associations; networking groups you are a member of; your competitors (within the legal, ethical and commercial boundaries of what is appropriate to debate with them); your sector-specialist media; the wider business media; and, of course, your customers;
- the next circle can be found online. The joy of the Internet is that potentially anyone in the world you would like to connect with is just a couple of clicks away. In the last few years, LinkedIn has become the go-to place to connect and using it wisely and effectively could merit a whole chapter beyond the scope of this book. We still come across CEOs who mistrust LinkedIn on the basis of a long-harboured resentment borne out

of its initial role as a recruitment platform, one reason being that a key person left a business they were running. Ditch all prejudices and dive in.

Aside from assiduously seeking the most appropriate connections, one great way to attract the sorts of thinkers and opinion-formers you would like to associate with and learn from is to publish your own thought piece on LinkedIn and see what comes back in terms of connection requests and below-the-line comments. This has proved to be a great way to lay down a marker and form the sorts of connections that may prove to be relevant and valuable. Let people find you rather than attempt to spam their way to attention with unwelcome or irrelevant connection requests.

So, in terms of cultivating 'outside-in' voices which can give you a constant flow of learning prompts, there has never been a better time in business than right now. As a result, the excuses for not forming circles of expansive connections are zero, it's time to build them now.

3.   Your tough love connections: here is where some bravery is required. In terms of a learning ecosystem, this can be the most effective anti-hubristic initiative. The most direct way to challenge pride and to moderate power is to make sure to pull into your sphere of influence those who will not be afraid to challenge and to question you. This is not in the spirit we talked about earlier of 'keeping your enemies closer'; it should not be as Machiavellian as that. This is about ensuring that you are always able to see any issue or policy decision from multiple angles prior to then being able to make an informed and well-rounded decision. It is about embracing plurality of thought, of others' outsider perspectives and the views of those you do not agree with.

We are referring to this as 'tough love', as opposed to 'tough questioning', as this input should be from connections whose questioning and probing is always underpinned with positivity and constructiveness. By all means allow raw honesty into the debate, but it should not be hostile and aggressive, which simply puts up the defences on both sides. Tough love is given in a spirit of positivity not negativity, and therefore is sustainable and ongoing.

Finding people who are prepared to conduct debate in that spirit is not easy. Such people need to be questioning but not cynical; honest but not abrasive; unafraid to speak out but ultimately respectful of a CEO's position and therefore accepting of your 'final say'. Cultivating and supporting such people in that role must never be patronizing, otherwise they will soon feel that they are little more than court jesters to be indulged by the king. Advisers who are prepared, consistently and honestly, to dole out tough love are therefore precious and a key skill for any CEO is to accommodate and nurture them.

Having that variety of voices informing you, however, is only of any real use if you listen to them. If, every time, the motive behind a listening exercise is to use it merely to harden an existing, entrenched viewpoint, then your tough love connections soon produce diminishing returns. Just using such people to confirm your prejudices or even for just the sport of a mighty disagreement will soon lead to those people being unwilling to express an opinion. In those circumstances, what may have started out as an anti-hubristic strategy has suddenly been turned into an aggressive form of hubris in its own right. Everyone else's opinion is sought only to be damned, buried and used as a vehicle to showcase the superiority of your own thinking. Think carefully about this cohort, as it has the potential to be the most important and sustaining part of your learning ecosystem.

4.   Your random connections: the final type of connection is one that, by its nature, cannot be planned or targeted. It springs from remaining constantly curious and open to ideas. By adopting such an outlook, you will notice and take advantage of connections that, almost instinctively, you believe may be of value in learning more or uncovering a fresh angle on things.

At trade shows, on the train or the plane, at the bar in a hotel catering for business delegates, somewhere, anywhere could be the most interesting person you are going to meet this year. Whatever your social style, you can find ways to create an introduction that feels totally comfortable for both parties. This only works if you enter into the conversation with no fast or opinion-seeking set agenda, just an enquiring and an open mind.

It is amazing how many stories one hears of happenstance, happy coincidences in terms of discovered shared connections, or downright luck that can lead to incredible conversations and networking opportunities. Done right, you can increase the odds for these things to happen, create the circumstances where it's regularly a small world in which just the people you need to meet present themselves. This is an art, not a science, and one that every truly great CEO has mastered.

Use your connections as your ecosystem

All your connections become your learning ecosystem and your commercial ecosystem. Just like any other system, this then requires tending, nurturing and feeding. Doing so in a way which is ongoing, creative and productive is, in itself, a leadership skill. Setting an example to your teams as an assiduous and effective networker is important. The world, your world, is in fact a small place when it comes to connecting effectively with the people you need to work with. Online has levelled the playing field, and has made it too easy for your competitors to emulate your carefully built-up set of connections. If you don't bother talking to the people that matter, they soon will, and you will diminish in their pecking order of people to consult and to network with.

Friendships and loyalties are hard to create and yet surprisingly easy to lose. 'I never seem to hear from that person these days' is not something that you want to hear from someone you value and whose opinions you respect. It may be said wistfully, even regretfully, but with every connection you need to understand whose court the re-connection ball is in. Someone may have said that about you, but it still may not be enough to get *them* to make the effort to reach out and make contact. In fact, quite the reverse; there could be some level of resentment at being neglected as a contact and a dog-in-the-manger attitude takes over: 'I'm going to leave it and just see how long it takes for them to make contact again.'

And, of course, you do not want to acquire a reputation for only making contact when you need something, like some neglectful college kid who only phones home when the money has run out. The best time to reach out and contact people is when you don't need something, not when you do.

Active networking and being open to new contacts and new meeting opportunities is a constant process, it never stops. Just as having a wide circle of friends enriches your personal life, so having an extensive range of learning contacts is one of the best ways to broaden, challenge and develop your business life. The nature and requirement of your set of connections should change and evolve, depending on which leadership phase you are in. Using the same three phases we referred to in Chapter 7, here are some recommendations on how to build and sustain connections in those three, very different, phases.

New leader phase connections

This is an interesting time, as your connections are both your strength and your weakness. If you have joined from outside the industry or sector, then you have some ground to make up compared with other CEOs in your sector, who already know all the movers and shakers. Is that necessarily a bad thing? You're the newbie in the established network, and maybe, just maybe, to start with you want to hold on to that outsider status for a while before jumping in and becoming part of the circle. It is not about being standoffish – it's evaluating where you want to fit before jumping straight in.

You also have a whole other dimension of connections that others do not have. People you know from your previous role may now prove to be rendered irrelevant or they might just be the most important people you need to know. Coming at things from an oblique angle, they (and you) may be the people who can strengthen your outsider perspective, or could be a surprising new collaborator or supplier into an established sector which is ripe for a shake-up.

With so many diverse opportunities to connect, it makes sense to assess the state of your connections and which category they fall into. Loosely, as well as the four categories we outlined above (buffer/ expansive/tough love/random) there are other headings under which each one may sit right now or may move into over time.

Take a good hard scroll through your virtual Rolodex (remember them?!) and make some cool decisions about the people on the list. I say 'cool' in the sense that this needs to be done dispassionately. From a business development point of view, there may well be connections that, in the nicest possible way, have served their purpose, but now, in your new role, it is time to move on. You do not have the luxury of carrying excess baggage into your new position. It's nothing personal – in the same situation, they may well do the same to you. Those held-over connections can end up being forced and hollow on both sides, so have the emotional intelligence to judge each one and decide whether to sustain that connection or to quietly let it drop.

The broad categories you may want to place people into are as follows:

- keepers: these are either friendships you value just as friends or where they provide buffer, expansive or tough love qualities to your relationship. In addition, as you are new here, these are outsiders, too, from your past world, so think about the value that brings;
- discarded: these are people who may never know that you have in any way actively discarded; it's just that you will no longer contact them on an active basis;
- targeting: these are people in your existing list of contacts, even as loose as a long-ago connection on LinkedIn with whom you have never

engaged in any meaningful dialogue, who, looked at from the fresh perspective of your new role, now seems to have acquired an extra level of relevance and value.

You may not have appraised your list of contacts in such a way for years, or indeed ever. Previously, it's just been a list to use or not use. Being in the new leader phase can be the perfect moment to conduct such an audit, so treat this as an essential part of the process of adapting to this new role. However cold it sounds as a process, it can end up being a warm reminder of which connections really matter, which have been neglected and which ones need to have some extra effort made to nurture and bring them back to life.

This is only half the process. There are all these new people to get to know. Meeting new people should always be one of the impulses for having taken on a new role. If you are not a 'people person' (whatever that tag means), then you will never be a fully rounded CEO. Even in a world of data and AI, it is still human connections that make the difference. 'Who you know, not what you know' is still as true as it ever was, as is 'people buy people'. Personality, charisma, charm and persuasiveness can never fully be quantified and certainly not listed on a balance sheet, but, even now, they can be a powerful competitive advantage. They may well be the qualities that ultimately secured the new role in the first place, ahead of qualifications and the notional quality of the CV. Use these same qualities to make all those important new connections. Legislators, trade bodies, suppliers, local stakeholders, customers – they are all susceptible to a charm offensive. This is not a smarm offensive, which is, well, offensive. It's bringing people onside, on your terms, for the good of the organization and in the interests of developing a genuine win-win relationship.

Embrace this connecting phase and at the same time bring your outsider perspective to every new relationship. It's not cosy; it's new and even bracing. Play the trick of being guarded yet open – this is certainly possible, even if it sounds like an oxymoron. Using all your experience, be a shrewd judge of character and decide who your allies will be as quickly as you can. Leveraging your connections, old and new, can be the difference between fast, effective progress in your new role or a desperate bid to get up to speed.

Successful CEO phase connections

By the time this phase has arrived, your list of meaningful connections will have been honed and refined. No longer an outsider, you will now be more reliant on your outsiders to provide those checks and balances for you.

New connections will likewise have been cultivated further or quietly discarded. This will have been an important process to go through, as making the assumption that so-and-so is not worth getting to know may be a piece of received wisdom in this sector that is based on misplaced prejudice or some now-forgotten event in the past. Take the trouble to form your own opinion about someone and have the courage to revise your opinion over time, too.

You can, however, afford to sharpen your focus, concentrating your meaningful connections on those which are tangibly aiding your judgement and informing your opinions. Success breeds success, and by now you know who is contributing to that and who is not. And there may well be some surprises, compared with initial impressions, on who it is that is helping to fuel that success. Being pleasantly surprised by someone is one of the best feelings, and one to be embraced.

During this phase, it is head down, focus on the winning team and run with it. The focus will inevitably be on strategy and execution, using the best people you know to help you to deliver this.

Established leader phase connections

It is now that you can lift your head again. There is time to draw breath and spend some time re-evaluating everything, including the profile of your connections. You know your team and they know you, you accommodate each other's foibles and ways of approaching things. There is a track record of trust and of accomplishment.

Now is the time to reach out once again. It is a time where fresh connections can contribute to reinvention, to a renewal of being challenged and being stretched, just what the established leader needs to stay fresh. If all the hard work, focus and energy expended in the previous phase has laid the foundations for a continuation of success, then a way to help to ensure continuing success, while at the same time avoiding complacency, is to seek new connections.

This can take time, but that time has been bought through an established bedrock of success. New connections can also help to guard against pride and hubris in this phase when there is most danger of that creeping in. Seek out those who will place your success in perspective rather than laud it, while at the same time avoiding sycophants who may want to be connected to you for their own gratification. By now you have the experience to sniff out such individuals and their motives.

Circle back around the process and decide again on keepers, discarded and targeted people. You are in a stronger position, so aim as high as possible. There may be people of power and influence who were, frankly, beyond your reach when you were new to the sector. But now, use your success to approach them as an equal. This is not pride or hubris, this is just plain fact. To deny it or be too modest and self-effacing may deny your organization access to a powerful potential ally or asset. The thing is, hubris is deeply unattractive, and can be smelled by those you seek out. Your self-aggrandizement will repel others, just as you have found it unattractive in relation to people seeking to connect to you.

Each phase requires self-awareness

The power dynamic at play in each phase between you and those you seek to connect with will change each time. Recognizing which phase you are in, embracing it and connecting in an appropriate way is a key skill. Ultimately, such recognition can make all the difference; it can be the factor which allows a CEO to progress smoothly from new leader to successful CEO and then on to established leader. If the right connections are not shrewdly cultivated, this particular career moment can come to a juddering halt.

The strength, quality and variety of connections, friendships and mentoring relationships can, in fact, end up being one of the main ways to judge success. Making a difference can be more about enriching the lives of the people around you through your connection to them than it can be about making improvements to the balance sheet. It can certainly be more satisfying and deep-rooted.

In the end, connections are everything. They are the difference between success that is short-lived and bought and one which is long-term and earned. No CEO, however clever, hard-working and resourceful, can achieve everything on their own. Those who believe they can have a hubristic mindset right there. Those who connect, share and listen are the ones who create the conditions for sustainable success.

3. Value diversity

The most important 'tough love' connections you can cultivate are right there with you in the boardroom. A CEO's nearest and most obvious set of advisers are the C-suite. As we have mentioned before, how this group is chosen, listened to and empowered is one of the main checks and balances that can be put in place. All should be independently minded people who are not afraid to stand up to a CEO and fight their corner. And, in turn, the CEO should not be afraid of such a team being in place, even if this means there is the prospect of being outnumbered in the boardroom.

We have looked at a few high-profile hubristic moments from the past few years, some of which have had fatal consequences, and all of which have inflicted serious reputational blows as well as financial damage to the companies involved. We have scrutinized the CEOs at the centre of some of these events but let us now imagine their C-suite members and some of the gnawing regrets they may have.

In a programme as central to the future of the company as the 737 Max was to Boeing, senior figures involved in detail in the software development and testing that led up to its launch will have had misgivings at the time. Did they voice their concerns, only to have them ignored and overruled, or were they supine and toed the party line until the nightmare unfolded? Similarly, who sat on their hands during the episode we described in Chapter 3, General Motors' replacement ignition switch debacle? Or colluded in the sanctioning of Uber's software designed to avoid giving rides to law enforcement officers in areas where Uber's services had been declared illegal? Or said nothing as Murdoch dismantled the trailblazing social media purpose of Myspace and turned it into just another media outlet, with disastrous financial consequences? The list of examples we have documented is varied and damning, and, of course, there are thousands of similar avaricious, hasty, ill-thought-out executive decisions being rubber-stamped every day in boardrooms around the world. A tragic few have fatal consequences; many others ruin businesses and the livelihoods of thousands of employees, suppliers and local communities.

If you are the CEO whose name is on those decisions, the buck, of course, stops with you, and we have seen the damaging effect of that. Strangely, it is probably those CEOs who, ultimately, sleep better at night than their respective C-suite members. At least those CEOs *acted*, however flawed their judgements may have been. They took a decision, they can rationalize to themselves, and, with all the known facts in front of them, they set about taking the course that they did.

A lifetime of regret

The C-suite members, though … what of their playback of events? If they opposed, warned, probed and argued to the best of their ability against a particular course of action, they will sleep easy. But what if they didn't? Does what they *didn't* do continue to nag away? Regret at not doing something is nearly always more painful than when you have tried something and failed, or even when you have done something that's a hideous mistake. At least something was *done*. In a different context, it's a bit like the saying, 'It's better to have loved and lost than never to have loved at all.' If something happened, then at least you can get over it. If something never happened when it should have done, that's much harder; replaying the endless 'what ifs' would drive most people to the edge of sanity.

The reason for looking at these types of events through the lens of C-suite members is to underline not just their duty to act and to call out CEOs when they are embarking on decisions which can be seen to be wrong, but to highlight the longer-term consequences. Anyone with a moral or ethical compass may, in the wee small hours of the morning, end up ruing their inaction long after any outward financial or reputational damage has been repaired. As such, from that side of the boardroom table, there is a duty to stand up and be counted.

Ensuring a diversity of views

As for the CEO, if rash or downright idiotic decisions are less likely if someone with a command of all the facts (or at least more of the detail) talks them out of such decisions, how exactly is that achieved when it is most needed? It is done by skilfully assembling the C-suite team – either putting together a new team when arriving in post or working with an inherited team, or a blend of the two. The first approach, as we have seen in relation to English Premier League football managers, can go in one of two ways. It is either the importing of a winning team, capitalizing on an approach and a style which has achieved results elsewhere; or it is a warning sign – an imposition of a team moulded and cast in the manager's own image which brooks no debate or dissent. A boardroom decision of this type needs to be studied carefully by non-execs and other instruments of governance to ensure that it is not going to lead to the total dominance of one voice, that of the CEO, at the expense of any checks and balances.

Assembling a team

If a team is being assembled rather than imported wholesale, putting it together successfully, *Magnificent Seven*-style, is one of the key skills of a great CEO. Finding the perfect blend of skills and attitudes that will achieve that synergy so elusive in many mergers and acquisitions is not easy. It is made harder for the CEO by the need to fight against what is easy. It is easy to find people eager to work for you who will toe the line every time and appear to be in awe and in agreement with you on an almost constant basis. What an easy life lies ahead with a team like that, and so tempting to succumb to.

Far more difficult is finding that sweet spot, the blend of the right people with the commensurate skills and wide-ranging knowledge who will also consistently challenge, question and demand more of you. Freethinkers who do not lack boldness in helping to arrive at strategic decisions and are also capable of channelling that boldness into challenging decisions. There is growing societal pressure for boards to reflect the diversity of their customers. A mix of gender and ethnicity and background which is more in line with the demographics of the client base is surely one to be welcomed. It is one step closer to understanding your customers and, indeed, all stakeholders. It also makes it more likely (although not inevitable) that a diversity of opinion will be more easily achievable with a more diverse team.

Without falling into the trap of virtue-signalling that we highlighted earlier in this chapter, making it known that the profile of the senior team is rich and diverse will invariably be popular with customers and with opinion-formers about your business, not least the media. Again, though, let this be judged by actions not words. Diversity on a board needs to be demonstrated by deeds in relation to issues such as the gender pay gap or clear opportunities for advancement based purely on merit rather than background.

Achieving a balanced team

It is common for incoming CEOs to appoint talented people to key strategic roles in their new organization. For many of us who have deployed this strategy ourselves, we can see why it makes sense. Having a 'go-to' trusted adviser in your midst, as you navigate unknown waters, provides a level of comfort and security. You know your team includes one or two trusted members who have your back and are committed to your success.

However, the risk here is that you may be blind to the depth of talent that lies before you. Hubris can be avoided by not making assumptions about people. Simply because you have not had direct experience with someone does not mean that they are less capable or trustworthy than those with whom you have deep ties. In other words, recognize the value in cultivating and developing a new cohort of team members. These individuals can bring to the table different, independent, insightful perspectives on a variety of issues that you might face.

Equally, if you find yourself up against a colleague now elevated to the heady heights of being the 'boss', recognizing that the nature of that relationship has changed will be critical when building a successful team. Too often, leaders can fall into the trap of believing that to establish their position as leader requires being more aloof, more standoffish, more outwardly confident and more self-assured. While it is important to establish from the outset that the relationship will be different, care is required in *how* this is done.

Achieving this balanced team membership from the outset is critically important. Investing in establishing a shared vision, providing insight into who you are as a leader and what you stand for, and setting the norms and cultural DNA for how the team models the values and behaviours that you want to see permeate the organization, are all important to establish and signpost from the outset.

One of the great misconceptions of both individual and team performance is that of perfection. We want to win, which results in a desire to overcome all possible weaknesses in pursuit of a 'perfect' performance. There's nothing wrong with winning, right? After all, we're in business to succeed, to crush the competition. We expect our people to deliver all the time and be better than the next guy. Winning is the goal … but at what cost?

We want flawless delivery, which means that we often see those who make mistakes as 'weak links'. We thin out the herd; we want them off the team. The common practice of ostracizing those who can't seem to deliver on high expectations means we plan to get rid of 'dead wood'. People start to avoid 'weak' players or work around them, which can create an environment of fear. No one wants to be seen as the one who made the mistake, nor wants to be the weak link. Mistakes are covered up, people start pointing fingers and blaming others. Fear becomes pervasive in the environment, and this leads to – you guessed it – the rise of hubris. Suddenly, ego-driven leadership takes the reins and, as they say, pride cometh before a fall.

There is a better way: safety. And here is how to achieve this hubris-killing, critical aspect of high performance.

Engender trust and co-operation
The first part of this is very simple: hubris cannot thrive in a shame-free environment, and there is no place for shame in honest, forthright collaboration where true co-operation is the sole aim. Bringing teams and groups together with a common aim, in an atmosphere where feedback is welcome, discussion is open and respectful, and everyone is charged with a collective outcome, means blame and shame find no place. There's true power when groups are brought together to work through their differences in support of each other and towards a common goal. This creates the perfect antidote to hubristic activity: trust.

Practise team behaviours

- Acknowledge mistakes as a learning opportunity for all – instead of singling out an individual, make it the group's responsibility to brainstorm a better way for everyone to move forward. Every perceived flaw is an opportunity to raise the group's performance. It's the old wartime concept of 'no man left behind'.

- Leaders must own up to their own perceived weaknesses and mistakes – by leaders openly admitting when they err, teams build trust and the ability to learn from humility. By openly discussing mistakes, leaders engender a feeling of camaraderie and collective performance progress. No one is to blame; everyone moves forward together.
- Open up the discussion – everyone can ask questions, curiosity is rewarded and problem-solving becomes a team effort.
- Practise blameless feedback – mistakes happen. Be sure to be curious about what happened in order to learn how such issues can be avoided in the future, but also ensure that dialogue is respectful, without blame or shame, and conducted in a spirit of collaboration.

Assessing internal team effectiveness

Just as we advocated earlier in this chapter, there is great value in conducting an honest assessment of the effectiveness of your team. Below is a set of questions that allows teams to benefit from a similar style of scrutiny that you yourself undertake. Think about the key teams that exist in your organization and ask a range of questions which can help to clarify their purpose, their effectiveness and the extent to which they foster co-operation and trust.

This can be a cascading exercise, with the CEO leading an assessment of the C-suite, specifically in relation to its effectiveness as a team. Then, each team further along the organization conducts a similar effectiveness audit. After all, it is often the case that teams come together and then remain in place long after the reason for them forming in the first place has been fulfilled or has changed. In the context of this assessment, teams may be regarded as being two different types, but in essence the scrutiny and reappraisals are as valid for each type:

1. Formal functional teams: a team brought together by role, by sector or by geography. Examples of these could be the C-suite

team; departmental heads across departments; or teams within a department.

2. Project teams: teams put together with a finite purpose relating to an initiative, a strategy or a tactic. Usually time-limited, with a specific objective.

Questions to ask within teams:

- Clarity of purpose. How well do team members understand their role? Is each member clear about their specific area of accountability? Indeed, is the purpose of the team as an entity regularly scrutinized and re-evaluated?
- Think about team meetings or online discussion forums. To what extent is there open discussion and the ability to challenge decisions? Does the team work together to achieve the best outcome? Conversely, what evidence is there of team members pursuing their individual interests at the expense of those of the team?
- Team leadership – to what extent as a leader do you ensure that everyone is given the opportunity to participate in group decision-making?
- Team self-sufficiency – does the team work to resolve issues themselves? Or is there regular recourse to external help?
- In that regard, is the profile of the team membership correct?
- Team democracy – assess the extent to which information is shared openly and is accessible to all team members.
- How comfortable do team members feel about raising dissenting views? What mechanisms are in place to empower this to happen?
- Further than that, are team members actively encouraged to push back and challenge opinions, decisions or a consensus?
- Evaluate the extent to which you test the level of tolerance to failure, by team members sharing their difficulties when mistakes or misjudgements have been made.
- Team leadership – as a leader, what role do you play? Are you an enabler and a listener, encouraging and facilitating discussion and debate? Or is that position used to impose a dominant viewpoint?

- As a leader, do you use the role to check on the wellbeing of all team members?
- Team sharing – is the allocation of tasks and responsibilities drawn up using a traditional view of seniority and experience? Or is the opportunity taken to nurture and develop talent by assigning roles to newer, less experienced members?

Just as a leader's honest assessment can highlight areas of weakness and scope for a change in approach and outlook, so a team which questions everything, even the validity of its own existence, can uncover some interesting truths.

Avoiding gridlock on the board

In Chapter 6 we discussed the balance between collaboration and urgency, of finding a broad and informed consensus, even if it takes time to arrive at the best decision. This conundrum is set up to exist if a board is assembled with an empowered and diverse set of voices all able to be heard. If board meetings become all wise debate and no decisions, a zeal for consensus has taken on too much importance. At the end of the day, the CEO must make a decision, made potentially harder by creating the circumstances where equally competing, cogent arguments have been put forward by the carefully assembled team.

The skill at this point is to weigh everything up and then deliver an informed judgement which cuts through all the argument and is seen, and accepted, by all as the best decision. The shrewd CEO will be able to balance debate with reaching a decision, and diverse views with achieving a consensus.

A board which speaks its mind

This happy balance requires patience, tolerance and perspective, something in short supply to a proud or hubristic leader. Even if the path of the new leader phase is paved with good intentions, with the appointment of a pluralistic board (and one that listens), all too often the steady and insidious erosion of a promising kick-off can start to occur. As the months pass, along with the honeymoon period itself, impatience settles in; there's a sense of going through the motions of listening and a hardening of attitude. You can see CEOs who play the board as a politician might: appearing to be caring and sharing but under it all pursuing a ruthless agenda of self-interest.

It is at this point that the board needs to heed the warning signs of what is occurring and fight back. Has the board stopped believing in the infallibility of the CEO? If the board finds itself agreeing with everything the CEO puts forward, either the CEO is a genius (unlikely) or has fooled the board into believing this to be the case (more likely).

4. Be truly coachable

It's one thing to coach others, but quite another to be coached and coachable, welcoming the opinions, scrutiny and oversight of others. CEOs and C-suite executives, indeed anyone in a position of power and authority, should be open to this process. The best mentors have mentors themselves, and if you are going to be a genuinely nurturing influence, as we have recommended above, you in turn need to be receptive to being nurtured yourself.

The first step in being coachable is establishing a willingness and desire to constantly learn. To do that requires us to confront and embrace the things that we don't necessarily do well. When we are not able to achieve what we want, how do we react and what behaviours are triggered? When the wheels come off the bus and look like they cannot be put back on, how do we react to mistakes and failures?

Difficult things are … well, difficult, and failure is part of life. There should be no shame in admitting failure, or struggling with challenges and decisions. Leaders who refuse to admit they are struggling may be encountering or experiencing full-blown hubris. It takes great self-confidence not to use power and influence to force compliance, and to humbly expose one's opinions to open debate. Humble executives focus on the larger vision and a broad set of stakeholders rather than their own ego. They listen to others, consider multiple points of view and do not assume their own opinions are infallible. Nurturing humility requires patience. It often takes time for a CEO to reflect on a decision rather than snatching at the most expedient solutions and self-serving explanations so common in narcissistic or dismissive cultures.

Learn from mistakes

To avoid these pitfalls, a great CEO needs to be unafraid. Unafraid of honest feedback, of being challenged and of receiving bad news. Surround yourself with people who demand more of you and do not resent it when that happens. None of this is easy; almost all of it is the opposite of the basic and understandable human impulses to be defensive, to be vain and to seek to put off confronting painful situations. This is where the value of the rewards package is put to the test. If all this was easy, anyone could do it, not just an elite at the apex of corporate life. Consciously diffusing power (because that is what is involved) is hard, particularly when power has been hard-won. Accepting criticism, being receptive to others' viewpoints, learning from bad situations, and conducting yourself with openness and honesty are all the hallmarks of a great leader. Turning negatives into positives does not just happen by refusing to face up to a negative, in fact quite the reverse. It is about embracing it, understanding it and learning from it, so as to avoid making the same mistake twice.

Don't apportion blame. If the first thing you ask when something goes wrong is 'Whose fault is this?' rather than first looking at your own role in the decision, something is wrong. If you put too much emphasis on accountability at the expense of problem-solving and solutions, we are back to the climate of fear where bad news is buried rather than fixed.

Solicit honest feedback anonymously

If constructive and open feedback has been successfully instilled in the boardroom, why stop with the C-suite team? If a climate of honest feedback has been fostered there through a wise selection of the characters in the team, this can be extended to the entire organization. This is easier said than done. While a fellow director might feel empowered to square up to the CEO and call out a failure of policy or strategy, it is far more difficult for a more junior employee to do the same. No matter how often or earnestly you assure employees that you welcome honest feedback, you are unlikely to receive any. Why would they risk putting their head above the parapet? There will always be an example, even from way back, of the time when someone spoke their mind and saw their career sidelined as a result. Who wants to end up like that? A system needs to be put in place where people feel free and comfortable in giving honest and constructive feedback. While the ideal is for the workplace to be 'psychologically safe' the reality is, that even when the feedback is anonymous, for this to work effectively there needs to be follow-up action and results. If feedback has been posted publicly, a response and any action and conclusion must be treated in the same way.

Keeping criticism and feedback constructive, while avoiding focusing it on personal attacks in our social media-trolling culture, is difficult but vital. All feedback conduits or forums do need to be moderated to some degree, even if this attracts criticism of censorship. This ends up being more to protect the posters from themselves and intemperate posts than as a management defence.

Leaders must also be willing to entrust other individuals with the role of delivering feedback on performance. Just as taking on board criticism or divergent views in the boardroom can be tough, this can be even more challenging. If you've made it as a CEO, regardless of which phase you are in, it can be easy to believe that your days of requiring coaching and mentoring are over. This may be part of the input that enabled you to get where you are, so surely all the lessons have been successfully learned and applied. The problem is that a whole new set of even more complex demands on your skills are now forced on you in the CEO role.

The effectiveness of a CEO can be measured in the length of time that an individual is willing to keep learning from others. The best mentors to turn to will be independent of the organization, people who can provide differing perspectives and an external view of problems and issues. To turn to such a resource is not a weakness; rather, like so much that we are recommending, it is a strength. The courage and the insight to be able to know that you don't have to be the smartest person in the room; that being inquisitive, an individual who constantly seeks to learn, is an outlook and practice that every CEO should yearn to follow.

Embrace bad news

To be coachable, you need to display and achieve balance and openness. This manifests itself in many ways, not least in terms of how bad news is handled. Bad news occurs daily in any large, complex organization, no matter how well run. It may be in the form of poor results, failed test products and prototypes, lost contracts, failed bids, bad debts, supplier failure, system crashes; the list is endless and we have probably all experienced some of those things at some point in our working lives. Such events are often compounded by coincidence and bad luck, meaning that you can have a run of bad news within a specific department or sector.

CEOs who build a culture of relentless positivity and a permanent focus on success go about branding all conveying of bad news as negativity, as if somehow it would all be a lot better if everyone had the right *attitude*. It's probably embodied in another motivational poster on the boardroom wall. This places the blame for poor results solely on behaviour rather than on events, and in this climate the main emotion when conveying bad news is fear: fear of failure, fear of retribution, or fear of humiliation in front of peers.

We're speculating here, as obviously we weren't present in any of the boardrooms of the companies featured in our earlier case studies. However, we believe that such fear is likely to have been at the root of many of the cover-ups and failures we have outlined. Cover-ups, as we have seen in the systems failures at Boeing and General Motors, and in the financial irregularities at Deutsche Bank, were often as harmful to these businesses as the events themselves. Where does this impulse to initiate a cover-up start? In the boardroom. If the first cover-up is the burying of bad news so that, 'if we're lucky, the CEO won't get to hear about it', we're definitely on a slippery slope.

If there is a culture of secrecy, evasion, half-truths and an avoidance of responsibility and accountability, this can soon become established at all levels of the organization. In this climate, denial and blame take hold, first within the business and then in communication beyond the company's walls. Commercial sensitivity and confidentiality become the smokescreen behind which everything is hidden. The now largely discredited (but still overused) legal instrument of non-disclosure agreements (NDAs) are used as gagging orders to suppress bad behaviour, as we have seen in recent high-profile #MeToo court cases.

All this is set in motion from the top. CEOs who suppress bad news often end up suppressing *all* news. Everyone becomes afraid to divulge anything more than is necessary, as they have seen that knowledge is power and that it should be exercised sparingly. Debate is stifled, collaboration is suppressed, all the virtues we have talked about are crushed out of the system by this filtering out of bad news. It's this situation that is the real bad news for a business.

A pebble in the shoe

Bad news will only ever get worse if it is suppressed or not acted upon. It becomes a corporate pebble in the shoe, making a journey more painful and difficult than it needs to be. You need to just stop and take the time and effort to remove it. The pebble will never simply work its way out: you have to stop, sit down, take off your shoe and shake it out. This always feels like a bit of a chore. When it's done, it is a blessed relief. But leave it where it is and you will get a blister, which will take time to heal.

And so it is with the corporate pebble. The longer it's there, hidden, the more it chafes, the more pain it causes, and the more it slows down progress. Instead of bothering to remove it, here the impulse to delay is driven by fear of failure. That metaphorical pebble, even if it came from outside the business and it was simply bad luck that caused its arrival, in a climate of relentless positivity it is seen as yet another negative; somewhere it's someone's fault. Stopping to remove it will be admitting that it even exists, so let's disguise our limp and struggle on.

Encourage debate

If you are encouraging feedback from all levels of the organization, and have created a culture where bad news can be aired without hesitation and where healthy debate is encouraged, one further step can be taken in the process of valuing diversity. The best word to describe this is nurturing. Nurturing others to explore possibilities, take decisions and assert real control, even at the expense of the CEO's own notional power base. These are all things that a hubristic executive is reluctant or unable to do. It requires a generosity of spirit and of time, spending this with others to share skills, expertise and wisdom. It is also about lifting, encouraging and supporting the achievements of others.

Approached correctly, nurturing others becomes a win-win. The recipients receive coaching and encouragement which, if the CEO is worthy of the position, comes from the best possible source anyone in that organization could hope to receive it. What's in it for the CEO? By surrounding themselves with a team which has benefited from their nurturing approach, that team will all be more effective, more motivated, more in tune with the CEO's ethos.

By taking on board all these strategies to encourage, value and nurture a diversity of opinion and outlook, the decision-making and strategy-setting of a business will be enriched and the conditions will be in place to minimize the chances of the sorts of hubristic decisions we have highlighted earlier in the book and which have damaged so many businesses, sometimes fatally.

5. Dismantle hierarchies

Most of us accept hierarchies as the norm when it comes to society and business. The concept of top-down leadership is something many of us never even think to question. It's just the way things are done. Or is it?

During the Industrial Revolution, hierarchies became normalized as businesses adopted a top-down means of accomplishing as many repetitive tasks as efficiently as possible. Leaders set forth the directive of how tasks would be done, which trickled down through layers of middle management who oversaw the individuals performing the work. Production and commerce have been organized in this way ever since; those at the top gather information, make decisions and hold the power, while workers at the bottom of the order are rewarded for conformity and unquestioning obedience.

Hierarchies, it seems, have been a long-accepted standard operating model of business and political success. Consequently adopted en masse, they've long been understood to be the means of maintaining an individual sense of purpose and a wider sense of organization and order. Establishing a hierarchy means there is an allotted place for those who wish to participate, and this orderly manner of things holds anarchy at bay. This has worked for over a century or more, as we have witnessed the rise of capitalism and the sheer power of top-down organizations to provide wages, municipal income, gross domestic product and structures of power within which men and women have built career aspirations.

It is when hubris is allowed to permeate a hierarchical structure that multiple problems can arise. Mistakes become hidden for fear of retribution or embarrassment; learning opportunities are hidden in exchange for a blame game. When hubris runs rampant within an organizational structure, pride is more important than principle and, despite the best intentions of the enterprise, chaos is likely to follow.

How to move from a hierarchy to an amoeba organization

Instead of relying on a traditional hierarchy, the key is to create fluid organizational structures, which provide accountability but also allow creative thought and action to flourish. There are a number of innovative ways in which these more fluid structures can be put in place.

For example, the creation of 'labs' where the potentially 'next big thing' can be developed and tested before it becomes a fixed specification or even an identified solution to an existing issue. Failure is not just part of the process; it is embraced as an essential and inevitable part of the journey to the next world-beating idea. Part of this also hinges on delegating responsibility to all parts of the business where ideas and talent then have the potential to grow and develop.

Create fluid teams

A related approach is to do away with a rigid and fixed demarcation between functions and departments, moving instead towards the concept of the amoeba organization. Set up in this way, people who are deployed on projects and initiatives are empowered to bring together the best individuals who will produce the best results. Just as on a macro level the organization should be embracing diversity and plurality, so within itself it is time to tear up old-style organizational charts. These have created too many boundaries, and too many harbours for vested interests and division. Ultimately, traditional hierarchies render businesses too slow to handle fast-paced business change. They destroy innovation and the ability to react creatively to change, while providing a breeding ground for closed decision-making and hubris.

How much better it is to have small, agile teams within a company which are self-organizing and are driving innovation and improvement through customer interactions and interesting cross-fertilization across a range of business disciplines. In such a set-up, the leadership team can focus on providing clear strategic intent and direction, providing a guiding light for its agile teams to follow.

This networked structure, as opposed to a single hierarchical one, enables more collaborative working both within and between teams. It becomes an organization that communicates company goals in an effective way and encourages co-operative working to achieve them. It fixes what we've illustrated below, commonly referred to as the broken triangle. The broken element is the line connecting company success with individual performance. In a traditional hierarchy, this is the side of the recognition triangle that is most likely to fail. When decisions are all imposed downwards, then the belief that, as a cog in the wheel, you can have any tangible effect or bearing on the success of the business becomes negligible. However, in an amoeba-style structure, every part of the organism has an intrinsic part to play in its survival, growth and success.

Personal Satisfaction
Personal Rewards

Source: David Cobb

The key additional part of the triangle, and the one which ultimately fixes it when it has been broken, is the introduction of co-operative working. By embracing this, individual performance is restored to a position of equal importance to that of company success. The triangle is whole again: the three elements of company success, individual performance and co-operative working are equal – in their importance and in their effect.

In order for co-operative working to be successful, there are five basic principles to be put in place:

1. Co-operative working is recognized, rather than just individual efforts.

2. Individuals are encouraged to appreciate that personal satisfaction comes from co-operative working.

3. Individual rewards are determined from contributions to the group effort.

4. There is no route to contribute to company goals other than through co-operative working.

5. There is no recognition or reward other than through co-operative working groups.

Of course, you still need managers and you still need rules; the world hasn't changed that much. However, in more flexible organizational structures, managers become enablers rather than enforcers. They become people who remove impediments rather than create them through bureaucratic practices. The challenge is for managers to become enablers and catalysts for the success of the network relationship between customer>employee>organization. In this way, they set up an ecosystem for positive engagement and true co-operation.

The key to successful leadership in agile organizations is striking a balance between alignment and empowerment. 'Alignment' can be overused in organizations as nothing more than a euphemism for top-down direction. The solution is to create a culture based on values, strategic intent, and in creating customer value. Articulated well and consistently, these three elements create a shared purpose within an agile organization.

6. Nurture aspiration

The importance of the role of executive leadership in the development and nurturing of personal growth has filled the chapters of many books. In spite of this spotlight on its importance, it is still the case that, when CEOs are asked about their biggest concerns around the future of their businesses, scarcity of talent continues to feature in the top three to five.

Why is it that developing talent, having a cadre of next-generation leaders in place, has proved to be so elusive? Leaders have been known to break into new markets or turn around the fortune of ailing companies, but have yet to show as a leadership cohort that the majority have cracked it when it comes to capacity-building as far as people are concerned.

Could it be symptomatic of a trait of hubris of not wanting to be surrounded by too many talented and capable people who may ask too many questions? Or fear that such individuals could prove to be far more capable and shine a spotlight on areas in which the senior managers are lacking? Is it a protectionist strategy to ensure the incumbent is not shown up by successors who espouse a clearer and more relevant purpose and set of values? If such blocking strategies are the real reasons for this reluctance to nurture and develop talent, then such pride, self-centredness and negativity are surely classic symptoms of hubris.

The more charitable interpretation is that few leaders argue that developing, nurturing and retaining talent is critical to business success; it is just that they fail to connect this logical and sensible conclusion to the need for them to play an active role in making it happen.

There are countless studies that show that the most effective executive leaders spend, on average, 30–40 per cent of their time focused on talent and on people. In our work with leaders at executive levels, when we quote that percentage we are often greeted with a look of incredulity. 'That's not really the case, is it?' 'How can we afford to spend that amount of time on people, when there are a zillion other critical strategic areas that demand our time and attention?'

Our answer to these questions is as follows. Capital and people are the two resources that represent the foundations for the business and, while having an abundance of capital might be sufficient for a period of time, in today's fast-paced and uncertain world it is those organizations that have nurtured and developed the best people that will outpace those that fail to grasp this. A further edge is achieved by constantly inspiring this talented cohort to bring their best to work, every day.

The companies of tomorrow will be those that grasp the concept that competitive advantage comes from how quickly you can assimilate change, understand data, and connect and correlate desires and trends to outpace others. And that, despite the amazing advances in computing and technology, the difference is not access to and use of technology, but people. Great people. As such, the CEO's role in nurturing talent can serve as an effective antidote to hubris. It becomes the CEO's distinct and unique advantage in business, as long as it is well understood and acted upon with foresight and determination.

As a leader, what are the hallmarks that demonstrate you are vested in nurturing and developing talent?

Own it – don't delegate it

Firstly, you must *own* talent development; you must see growing future leaders as an organization-wide priority that has you and your stewardship firmly behind it. To own talent development, you must be able to articulate clearly what talent development means for your company. It must permeate every part of your cultural fabric, from the systems that are designed to support talent process through to the behaviours and actions you display and enact as a role model. It is not sufficient simply to espouse that talent management is important. You must be clear what it means to be a leader, and you must be intimately involved in all aspects of the process of growth and development of talent.

To nurture aspiration, you must first be clear on what your expectations are for a leader. This is not merely the technical capabilities that they bring to the table, but the core values that they must possess to be successful. The other trick is not to fall into the trap of 'They must be like me'. In previous chapters we have shown how a plurality and diversity of views could have been key to preventing some of the worst mistakes in modern corporate history. Hubristic leaders fail to listen to wise counsel or are unable to recognize, until it is too late, an overreaching, a cutting of corners, or a missed opportunity.

Set the direction and frame its importance

For the nurturing and developing of talent to be effective, it is important to set a clear example from the very top. The CEO and the C-suite must not only actively encourage people to develop their potential, they must actively be seen to be doing so. And the importance this holds as a key part of ensuring the future growth of the business must be clear to all as well.

Processes to adopt

Active stewardship of your organization's people processes matters. The growth and development of people must be as important an agenda topic as how the business is performing. To check if this is a reality in your business, here is a set of questions. Answer these truthfully in order to see where you are and where you need to get to in relation to this critical issue. How do you stack up when it comes to the following attitudes and processes?

Do you:

- Promote disciplined regular processes that engage in talking about the people in your organization?

- Seek to develop ways to expand and stretch people through discussion that is not simply going through the motions, but is an active dialogue with accountabilities and actions that are tracked over time?
- View talent from a perspective that moves beyond traditional performance v. potential measurements, that instead focuses on viewing talent through multiple lenses and from angles which align with short-term, long-term and those critical in-the-moment strategic objectives?
- Hold frequent dialogues more than once or twice a year? For example, do you host conversations at least quarterly that are focused and address specific development objectives?
- Insist on robust discussions that focus on asking challenging questions?
- Evaluate leaders' commitment to talent by assessing the value they place on developing and nurturing talent? A way to assess this is to scrutinize how leaders behave in specific circumstances. Examples might include: how willing a person is to offer their people for other positions; are they strengthening the organization through the track record of the quality of the people that *they* hire? How resourceful are they when times are tough? Have they sought the easy option that delivered results but damaged the long-term position?
- Align your culture so that there is a continuous process in place of active learning by leaders and their teams?

Inspire others by what you say and what you do

This whole area is one where leading from the front, creating an example for others to follow, is critical to success. Busy managers will always claim that time spent developing and nurturing talent inevitably gets squeezed out by day-to-day operational pressures and the more immediate commercial concerns of the business. This so-called alibi can be comprehensively overruled by the CEO demonstrably being able to carve out time and focus, on a consistent basis, for this longer-term goal. Build this up as a documented track record of behaviour, to be used where necessary, to dismiss excuses and delay in the behaviour of C-suite members and other managers in relation to nurturing talent.

Some examples of demonstrating a commitment to nurturing growth could be:

- engaging and getting to know your people is seen to move from merely pressing the flesh to proactive engagement;
- purposeful conversations that are set up that enable you and others to get to know and hear from those who are making valuable and important differences;
- knowledge of people and their capabilities moves beyond just knowing the leaders that report to your direct reports; instead, you have a solid grasp of the talent pool and familiarity with those deeper within the organization.

Investment in development is reflected in the time, resources and opportunities the company commits to in enabling people to expand and enhance their capabilities. People see you demonstrating the value of self-awareness by sharing your own learnings and vulnerabilities in interactions and discussions, and in turn link these to the value of a learning culture.

Let us now spotlight two specific groups that we urge CEOs not to ignore: the executive team and the board. These two teams are often best placed to spot the warning signs of hubris and ensure it is promptly nipped in the bud before it can cause any real damage.

Spotlight: executive and board team

Committed CEOs stewarding the process, powerful as they may be, can find themselves hampered if the actions of the teams below them don't mirror or reflect the same level of commitment or accountability. It's not dissimilar to discovering that the foundation that you built your house on is not fit for purpose. Structurally, it becomes unstable and eventually the cracks start to appear when it finds itself under stress.

It is time and investment that can make the difference. This may sound simple, but the truth is that if things are set up right at the start, it can become second nature and a part of your normal operating rhythm. The measurable impact is much greater. The benefits of investing in the nurturing of the executive team are many, not least of which is that within this group a potential successor may exist.

As a team:

- do you carve out time so that dedicated focus is placed on building and developing the individual and the collective capabilities of the executive team?
- is the team one in which it becomes habitual to provide feedback to each other as a regular meeting norm?
- do you demonstrate and recognize the value of those who are generous with new knowledge by sharing it with others, and promote knowledge as power to be shared?
- to what degree have you invested in developing capabilities to assess talent?

As a leader:

- do you engage in real-time and continuous feedback with each of your direct reports?
- to what degree do you encourage leaders and teams to hone and develop their own mentoring skills?
- how important do you think it is for leaders to spend time developing and honing their mentoring skills?
- in what ways do you look to provide the right avenues for executives to develop and enhance their capabilities?
- how willing are you to make the tough 'people decisions', and what do you take into account when making this call?
- whose responsibility do you think it is to develop capability: the company's, individuals' or leaders', or some combination of all three?

Measurement matters

We should not forget, however, that you can only determine how good the processes and practices in place are by the results and impact that they have. Just refer back to our earlier commentary about the number of CEOs who openly admit their concern about the dearth of talent in their organizations. All will have practices and processes in place, true; many may not have all of those that we encourage them to adopt, but the last critical area that we strongly urge leaders to put in place is a way of measuring the impacts and outcomes of their efforts. With the same rigour that is applied to measuring and holding people to account for the financial numbers, people should be accountable for nurturing.

This does not have to be complicated or include reams of data – far from it, in fact. Make the measures simple but clear. Ultimately, in the implementation of all these processes and practices, your goal is to make people be accountable for their actions.

There are some simple things that leaders ought to keep in mind:

- you're here to help people be heroes;
- you don't just care about people, you *get* them … and in turn, you get the best from them;
- you know good feedback is a gift – an ongoing way to motivate people to unleash their talents, to be the best they can be for themselves and for the company;
- by connecting people to opportunity, you show how much you trust them;
- you not only seek out talent, you liberate it;
- you're balanced – you know when to praise and when to have hard conversations;
- you bring an 'A' game to developing people.

7. Embrace self-reflection

Whichever phase a CEO is in, be it the learning new leader, the period spent consolidating success, or the confident, established phase, there's a danger in believing too eagerly your own press cuttings. It is, of course, fun to win awards, to be recognized in the media, and to become well known and referenced in your industry. This can lead to prestigious, high-profile appearances on television and online media. People start seeking you out to give talks, to provide insightful comment on events in the news, to be an expert who people turn to, and even be a representative spokesperson for issues in your sector.

It can be easy and beguiling to be swept along by all this attention; it can be heady, inspiring and motivating. But it can also turn into an emotional high that searches out more attention and plaudits to keep it satisfied. It can too often lead to hubris, as people find themselves wanting and needing more attention to maintain that attention high. Focus more on internal and external articles criticizing, second-guessing, or questioning your decisions. Pay attention to whether you feel contemptuous of your critics or humbled by them. Someone who is openly contemptuous or even vengeful towards their critics is more likely to be on the path to full-blown hubris.

Having said that, the media, in all its forms, social media included, can be a harsh environment in which to engage. Everyone is now an armchair critic, a keyboard warrior with the potential to undermine and demean anyone who holds power and influence. Even the mainstream business media can be capricious, setting people up for a fall, and individuals can move from flavour of the month to media pariah in the space of a single opinion piece. Signing up to a media profile therefore has both its thrills and its dangers.

In the previous section we cautioned against secrecy and a closed attitude, so getting out there and embracing media opportunities is certainly within the spirit of being open and available. And, used wisely, it can offer a huge competitive edge. Opinion-forming column inches in the business press, or anywhere your customers are seeing you, can be far more valuable (and essentially free publicity) compared with any amount of paid advertising. If you are the go-to person in your sector to comment on any issues affecting the stakeholders in your business, then every appearance, every opportunity to set the agenda rather than follow it, can be a big win over your competitors.

But again, in the wee small hours, take a moment to be self-reflective, and treat all the attention as a bit of a game, a fleeting circus which is not to be taken too seriously as a barometer of your true worth. Keep your feet on the ground and don't believe the hype (especially your own), otherwise all that media attention can grow you wings as unreliable as Icarus's, with similar consequences. If your own vanity doesn't eventually bring you crashing to earth, then the capricious nature of the media may well do it for you at some point. Better to play the media game all you can but not to value celebrity status for its own sake. If playing the game sounds cynical, then in this arena a healthy dose of cynicism, or at least realism, is what will keep you, and those around you, sane and grounded.

Find time for self-reflection

Earlier in this book we shone a spotlight on various companies and individuals whose success reached a point where narcissism and self-regard took over and removed any sense of perspective or control. A further example is Daimler-Benz, which had been so successful in the 1980s that its leaders developed a feeling of invincibility and arrogance. And then the inevitable occurred, just as industry experts had predicted. During the 1990s, the organization's performance suffered and deteriorated as a direct result of the arrogance displayed by some of its leaders.

The unrestrained growth of the company's aerospace division was presided over by Jürgen Schrempp, who later became CEO. He had a growing realization that the collapse of the company's fortunes was as much driven by internal issues as it was the result of the decline in the European economy. In previous shareholder statements, responsibility had been apportioned solely on such external factors.

Schrempp intervened to reinvent the company, taking personal accountability for the failures in the aerospace division and the ensuing bankruptcy. This resulted in the share price appreciating by 45 per cent over 12 months. Such honest and thoughtful reflection had resulted in the sort of reinvention often only made possible by bringing in someone new. He had ignored the politicians' maxim of 'Never complain, never explain' to do exactly that, and stakeholders responded positively. Reflection should be regarded as a structured, focused and conscious process of self-discovery and knowledge, which we undergo in order to develop a deeper understanding of ourselves. At the same time, it develops into the pathway for behavioural modification and change.

The practice of reflection and introspection is fundamental to learning from our experiences and forms the underlying process of how we learn and change our behaviour through coaching. By raising awareness of why we might think and behave in a specific way, we are able to make conscious decisions to change those thoughts and behaviours that may no longer be serving us well.

Strangely, hubris can develop as a defence mechanism by which individuals seek to protect themselves from feelings of humiliation or shame associated with the threat of exposure of character or skill limitations, either perceived or real. This lack of awareness means they are likely to avoid focusing on – or even developing – their limitations, which means there is no opportunity for these weaknesses to become strengths. Pride becomes a barrier to learning. A process of reflection is challenging for any proud individual, as they risk exposing themselves to vulnerability and to feelings that they actively avoid and are unwilling to confront.

Taking a step back to look at the bigger picture is often the important first step towards self-reflection. That may be honestly reflecting on the past track record of a business, such as Schrempp performed on Daimler-Benz, or it can be more grounded in personal history. It may be about considering and identifying what it is that we want from our lives and whether the way that we are currently operating is creating the conditions in which we can achieve a true, lasting legacy from our career. We have dwelt a fair bit on the need for values and purpose within a business. The vital associated step with this is for CEOs to find the time and space to reflect on their own values and purpose and ensure that these are aligned with their personal and professional goals.

CHAPTER 9

Conclusion: Conquering Hubris

As we look at the world today, we can see that leaders have a larger role to play on the global stage. It is no longer good enough to focus solely on how much profit you can generate, how big you can grow your company and how much you are able to court your shareholders or Wall Street. These are fine as key performance indicators – KPIs, to use the jargon – but the clue is in that phrase. They are merely judging performance; they are not judging purpose.

Nowadays, increasingly, the world is yearning for leaders who will not just lead but will play an active role in shaping the future.

To be such a leader carries great power but also great responsibility. A leader should only embark on the path of leadership if they truly know what they are signing up for.

Let us be clear: there is no perfect leader, no one person to whom we can point who has it all. The list of ideal attributes and requirements is a long one, as the one below demonstrates. In this book we have aimed, by scrutinizing high-profile leaders and some of the glaring hubristic events of recent corporate history, to illustrate ways in which we can all learn from such case studies to avoid some common pitfalls. And in the second part of the book we outlined some of the attitudes and strategies required to avoid hubris and to be the sort of leader required to navigate the complexities of the 2020s and beyond.

In this concluding section, we set out a set of abilities that, if embraced, can be a positive set of guides to great leadership:

- the ability to connect personal values and purpose to a company's vision and purpose;

- the ability to create, develop and mentor teams that are energized to deliver great things;
- the capability of capturing hearts and minds in good times and bad;
- the resilience and comfort level within one's own skin to be humble, decisive, bold and clear, all at the same time;
- the ability to be open to rawness, where you not only expose your own fears and vulnerabilities but actively look for that rawness to be exposed regularly through seeking honest and candid feedback;
- where your first action in building capacity is to look to hire, develop and surround yourself with people who are better than you;
- where the exhilaration that comes from knowing that it might have been your idea, your insight or your boldness that led to a great success was in fact not simply the result of your contribution, but also the result of all the other factors that enabled that great outcome to happen;
- where you stand up for a societal change that may rock the boat with those whom you rely on for endorsement, for profit or for investment, but yet you know deep down must be addressed. Having such a strength of purpose matters and cannot be merely brought out and paraded when it feels OK to do so;
- to be capable of genuine, heartfelt self-reflection, leading to a timely reappraisal of direction and purpose.

This last point is perhaps the most telling. The way to be a great leader and to avoid those hubristic tipping points which can confront every successful leader during their careers is to value self-reflection above all else.

Self-reflection is the ultimate weapon for guarding against hubris. Cultivating the ability to scrutinize yourself objectively and to remind yourself of your true values and purpose should be your guiding star.

Appendix: Conduct Your Personal Leadership Assessment

As an extra, included here is a bit of a hubris truth game. This is an opportunity to conduct an honest assessment of your leadership style and behaviours. Is your organization one in which the safeguards and checks are in place to ensure that the CEO and the board are performing in a way which is non-hubristic, is collaborative and is sharing in its outlook?

The best way to assess this is to look at a series of benchmarking criteria, which together form useful indicators as to the dominant culture currently in place. If you are a CEO, or an aspiring one, take a good, long, honest look at yourself and your current attitudes and methods of working, and see how closely you match up to this list of core capabilities.

How self-reflective, collaborative and inquisitive is the working life of your business? In what ways do the behaviour and actions of the CEO and the C-suite reflect and advance the values and purpose of the business?

As a way of checking the position right now of your organization and its CEO, particularly in relation to all seven of the better ways to lead identified in Chapter 8, take a look at the bullet points below and answer honestly, YES or NO, to this series of indicators of behaviour. Feel free to mark up these pages! Put a date on the page, too, and then revisit this list in six months' time to see if the dial has shifted.

Behaviours reflecting values and purpose

These can be divided into sub-sections:

The environment

- is reducing the impact of your business's activities on the environment a high priority in your organization?

  YES   NO

- if so, are there targets and actions to reduce that impact?

  YES   NO

- are environmental commitments an agenda item at every board meeting?

  YES   NO

- is a C-suite member specifically responsible for environmental issues?

  YES   NO

Fairness and Equality

- does the profile of the C-suite reflect societal ratios:

  of gender?

  YES   NO

  of ethnicity?

  YES   NO

- if not, are there plans in place to bring the organization closer to those ratios?

  YES   NO

- is there a gender pay gap in your organization (i.e. more than single digit percentage)?

  YES   NO

- if so, are there targets and actions to reduce this?

  YES   NO

- CEO to worker median pay ratio, a broad average is 100:1. Are there targets and actions to narrow this ratio in your organization?

  YES   NO

- are issues of fairness and equality an agenda item at every board meeting?

  YES   NO

- is a C-suite member specifically responsible for issues of fairness and equality?

  YES   NO

Charity and community

- does your organization have active partnerships with nominated charities?

  YES   NO

- does your organization have active links with local community organizations?

  YES   NO

- is a C-suite member specifically responsible for issues relating to charity and community?

  YES   NO

Collaborative behaviours

- does the CEO treat the board as an advisory function?

  YES   NO

- does the CEO have in place an advisory pool, drawn from a healthily, diverse range of sources: the board, employees, suppliers, customers, or other external sources?

  YES   NO

- is the executive decision-making process achieving an optimum balance between consultative richness and an efficient timespan?

  YES   NO

- is the rationale for key decisions shared with relevant stakeholders?

  YES   NO

- are there clear decision-making structures in place? Documenting them is easy to overlook and doing so is a great way to expose any gaps in a logical chain of command.

  YES   NO

Reflective behaviours

- are decisions relating to projects seen as a process, i.e. there is evidence that they continue to be reviewed, checked and monitored for efficacy over time, beyond the original decision.

  YES   NO

- outside of crunch points when decisions need to be made, is time and space set aside for reflection, analysis and contemplation?

  YES   NO

- are plans and strategies subject to a continuous state of review and reappraisal?

  YES   NO

- or are plans set in stone and only reviewed, say, annually?

  YES   NO

- does the CEO exhibit behaviour consistent with a level of self-doubt? If so, this is a positive, not a negative, as it demonstrates a questioning and reflective attitude.

  YES   NO

Inquisitive behaviours

- are you widely read on trends, demographics and cutting-edge developments, in your sector and beyond?

  YES   NO

- are you in the habit of firing out inquisitive 'What do we know about this?' emails with accompanying links, however random seeming?

  YES   NO

- is there active use of a one-page at-a-glance dashboard page of key metrics, updated daily?

  YES   NO

- is the boardroom a forum for open and honest feedback?

  YES   NO

- do C-suite members challenge decisions in a meaningful way?

  YES   NO

- is there an active use of satisfaction surveys or more discreet ways of canvassing opinions and feedback? These seek honest opinions from all relevant stakeholders: staff, customers, suppliers, industry bodies, sector opinion-formers.

  YES   NO

- if research is conducted, what is done with it? Is there a suitable follow-up process, including a response mechanism to survey respondees?

  YES   NO

- are you getting out and about? 'Management by walking about' is not just a cliché, it is a sound principle. Do the CEO and the board work on the basis that the office is an ivory tower, to be escaped from regularly? Visit departments, branches, customers and suppliers to find out what is really going on. Visit as often without an agenda as with one, to ensure that the widest range of topics is covered and aired.

  YES   NO

- are you unafraid to ask awkward/stupid questions? In fact, there is no such thing as a stupid question, as often a glaring flaw is only exposed by asking what may seem obvious.

  YES   NO

Connecting behaviours

How healthy looking is your circle of connections? Drawing on the categories of connection we outlined on pages 165–70, rate the breadth of your connections now and then circle back to this in six months' time. A target number has been placed against each category which may be regarded as a minimum working number. Feel free to adjust to your own, possibly more stretching, targets!

- your buffer connections – more than six?

  YES   NO

- your expansive connections – more than 20?

  YES   NO

- your tough love connections – more than 10?

  YES   NO

- your random connections – more than three per month?

  YES   NO

- have you conducted a connections audit in the past three months?

  YES   NO

- if 'NO' to previous question, do you plan to conduct a connections audit in the next three months?

  YES   NO

Have you marked up an honest response? If those marked YES outnumber those with NO, then the organization is probably sitting in the right area in relation to be equipped to make decisions that are balanced and considered. If the scoring is the other way around, then it is time to initiate a survey! You need to gather and analyse some attitudinal data relating to how valued and consulted people feel in relation to decisions which directly affect them.

If most of these behaviours and procedures are in place, then there are checks and balances in place in the conduct of the CEO and of the wider business, which indicates that hubris cannot flourish and spread. None of this will bend an organization out of shape and leave it at a competitive disadvantage. Quite the reverse, it will indicate that it is in a healthy place to tackle the fast-developing challenges that face us all.

Acknowledgements

We extend our gratitude to Brian Cullinan for providing the opportunity to attend Hollywood for its 89th Academy Awards, a front-row seat to Tinseltown's hubristic, poisonous culture that inspired this cautionary tale; Brandon Victor Dixon, Chase & Status, Gorgan City, KT Tunstall, Roger Sanchez, Jermain Dupri, Jesse McCartney, and the parliamentarians wishing to remain anonymous for candidly sharing your insights and experiences; Allie and Matt – our editorial team at Bloomsbury – for their commitment and willingness to extend deadlines, repeatedly; and lastly, Bloomberg, the BBC, the *Economist, Forbes, Harvard Business Review, MIT Sloan Management Review*, the *New York Times*, Sky News, the *Sydney Morning Herald*, the *Telegraph*, and the *Washington Post*, for engaging with us and sharing our work with the world.

Index